# WINTER CLIMBS: GLEN COE

### SELECTED SNOW, ICE AND MIXED ROUTES IN A TWO-VOLUME SET

**by Mike Pescod**

JUNIPER HOUSE, MURLEY MOSS,
OXENHOLME ROAD, KENDAL, CUMBRIA LA9 7RL
www.cicerone.co.uk

Mike Pescod 2022
Eighth edition 2022
ISBN: 978 1 78631 100 9
Seventh edition 2010
Sixth edition (by Alan Kimber) 2002
Fifth edition (by Alan Kimber) 1994
Fourth edition (by Alan Kimber) 1991
Third edition (by Ed Grindley) 1981
Second edition (revised by H MacInnes) 1974
First edition (by IS Clough) 1969

Printed in China on responsibly sourced paper on behalf of Latitude Press Ltd
A catalogue record for this book is available from the British Library.
All photographs are by the author unless otherwise stated.

 © Crown copyright 2022 OS PU100012932

### Updates to this Guide

While every effort is made by our authors to ensure the accuracy of guidebooks as they go to print, changes can occur during the lifetime of an edition. Any updates that we know of for this guide will be on the Cicerone website (www.cicerone.co.uk/1100/updates), so please check before planning your trip. We also advise that you check information about such things as transport, accommodation and shops locally. Even rights of way can be altered over time. We are always grateful for information about any discrepancies between a guidebook and the facts on the ground, sent by email to updates@cicerone.co.uk or by post to Cicerone, Juniper House, Murley Moss, Oxenholme Road, Kendal, LA9 7RL.

**Register your book:** To sign up to receive free updates, special offers and GPX files where available, register your book at www.cicerone.co.uk.

*Card sleeve:* Climbing Minus One Gully, Ben Nevis (photo: Hamish Frost)
*Front cover:* Climbing The Great Gully, Garbh Bheinn

# CONTENTS

Topos key . . . . . . . . . . . . . . . . . . . . . . . . . . . . . . . . . . . . . . . . . . . . . . . . . . 4
Preface . . . . . . . . . . . . . . . . . . . . . . . . . . . . . . . . . . . . . . . . . . . . . . . . . . . . 5

**INTRODUCTION** . . . . . . . . . . . . . . . . . . . . . . . . . . . . . . . . . . . . . . . . . . . 7
Winter climbing: a recent history . . . . . . . . . . . . . . . . . . . . . . . . . . . . . . 9
Types of winter climbs: snow, ice and mixed . . . . . . . . . . . . . . . . . . . 12
Weather . . . . . . . . . . . . . . . . . . . . . . . . . . . . . . . . . . . . . . . . . . . . . . . . 28
Avalanches . . . . . . . . . . . . . . . . . . . . . . . . . . . . . . . . . . . . . . . . . . . . . 35
Access . . . . . . . . . . . . . . . . . . . . . . . . . . . . . . . . . . . . . . . . . . . . . . . . . 37
Equipment . . . . . . . . . . . . . . . . . . . . . . . . . . . . . . . . . . . . . . . . . . . . . 38
Additional safety precautions . . . . . . . . . . . . . . . . . . . . . . . . . . . . . . . 40
Using this guide . . . . . . . . . . . . . . . . . . . . . . . . . . . . . . . . . . . . . . . . . 40

**GLEN COE** . . . . . . . . . . . . . . . . . . . . . . . . . . . . . . . . . . . . . . . . . . . . . . 47
          Aonach Eagach . . . . . . . . . . . . . . . . . . . . . . . . . . . . . . . . . . 51
**Buachaille Etive Mòr** . . . . . . . . . . . . . . . . . . . . . . . . . . . . . . . . . . . . . 55
          Stob Dearg . . . . . . . . . . . . . . . . . . . . . . . . . . . . . . . . . . . . . . 55
          Stob Coire Altruim . . . . . . . . . . . . . . . . . . . . . . . . . . . . . . . . 69
**Lairig Eilde** . . . . . . . . . . . . . . . . . . . . . . . . . . . . . . . . . . . . . . . . . . . . . 71
          Sròn na Lairig and Eilde Canyon . . . . . . . . . . . . . . . . . . . . . 71
**The Lost Valley (Coire Gabhail)** . . . . . . . . . . . . . . . . . . . . . . . . . . . . 74
          Lost Valley Buttresses . . . . . . . . . . . . . . . . . . . . . . . . . . . . . . 76
          East face of Gearr Aonach . . . . . . . . . . . . . . . . . . . . . . . . . . 82
**Coire nan Lochan** . . . . . . . . . . . . . . . . . . . . . . . . . . . . . . . . . . . . . . . 89
          North-west face of Gearr Aonach . . . . . . . . . . . . . . . . . . . . . 89
          Stob Coire nan Lochan . . . . . . . . . . . . . . . . . . . . . . . . . . . . . 91
          Far Eastern Buttress . . . . . . . . . . . . . . . . . . . . . . . . . . . . . . 106
          North face of Aonach Dubh . . . . . . . . . . . . . . . . . . . . . . . . 109
**Coire nam Beitheach** . . . . . . . . . . . . . . . . . . . . . . . . . . . . . . . . . . . 114
          West face of Aonach Dubh . . . . . . . . . . . . . . . . . . . . . . . . . 115
          Bidean nam Bian . . . . . . . . . . . . . . . . . . . . . . . . . . . . . . . . 122
          Stob Coire nam Beith . . . . . . . . . . . . . . . . . . . . . . . . . . . . . 129

**GLEN COE – OUTLYING AREAS** . . . . . . . . . . . . . . . . . . . . . . . . . . . 135
          Beinn Udlaidh . . . . . . . . . . . . . . . . . . . . . . . . . . . . . . . . . . 136
          Sgùrr na h-Ulaidh . . . . . . . . . . . . . . . . . . . . . . . . . . . . . . . . 142

|   |   |   |
|---|---|---|
|   | Beinn a' Bheithir | 142 |
|   | Beinn Fhionnlaidh | 144 |
|   | Garbh Bheinn | 145 |
|   | Stob a' Ghlais Choire | 147 |
| **Appendix A** | Useful contacts | 148 |
| **Appendix B** | Route summary table by area | 149 |
| **Appendix C** | Route summary table by style | 163 |

### Warning

Mountaineering is a dangerous activity carrying a risk of personal injury or death. It should be undertaken only by those with a full understanding of the risks and with the training and experience to evaluate them. Mountaineers should be appropriately equipped for the routes undertaken. Whilst every care and effort has been taken in the preparation of this guide, the user should be aware that conditions, especially in winter, can be highly variable and can change quickly. Holds may become loose or fall off, rockfall can affect the character of a route, snow and avalanche conditions must be carefully considered. These can materially affect the seriousness of a climb, tour or expedition.

Therefore, except for any liability which cannot be excluded by law, neither Cicerone nor the author accepts liability for damage of any nature (including damage to property, personal injury or death) arising directly or indirectly from the information in this guide.

## Map and topo symbols

|  |  |
|---|---|
| ———————— | route |
| ———   ——— | intersecting route |
| ▬▬▬▬▬▬▬▬ | approach route (map) |
| - - - - - - - - | obscured route |
| ▪▪▪▪▪▪▪▪▪▪▪▪ | route (not described) |
| - - - - - - - - | ascent and descent route |
| ① | route number |
| ● | route number (route not described) |
| ⓔⓡ | escape route |

# PREFACE

Winter climbing in Scotland is all about adventure. We are never quite sure what to expect each time we venture into the mountains, and variations in conditions and weather make every day unique. This uncertainty of outcome is what makes winter climbing so rewarding. The route descriptions in this guide should be taken on this basis; they are sufficient to follow the line of the climb, but climbers will be required to make decisions for themselves while on the route.

This book is not intended to be a definitive guide to all the climbs recorded in the region. For a definitive list of routes covering the area, readers are advised to consult the Scottish Mountaineering Club's series of comprehensive guidebooks, and the yearly *Scottish Mountaineering Club Journal* which contains details of new routes.

Instead, this book aims to be more than just a list of climbs. It attempts to guide climbers to the right climb for them on the right day, given the prevailing weather and climbing conditions. This is a new direction for winter climbing guidebooks and I hope it is useful to new and experienced climbers alike.

As always, your feedback is welcome. Descriptions are always evolving; we continue to build and share knowledge, and your comments will be gratefully received.

Good climbing.

*Mike Pescod, IFMGA Mountain Guide*

*Fort William, 2022*

*Late season snow cover on Tower Gap, Ben Nevis*

# INTRODUCTION

*The view towards Garbh Bheinn from Stob Coire nan Lochan, Glen Coe*

Scotland is world-renowned for its adventurous climbing, the scale of which reaches far beyond the modest scale of its mountains. There is a strongly defended tradition of climbing style that maintains the adventurous nature of the challenge. This style also ensures that we raise our standard of climbing to meet the challenge, rather than bringing the challenge down to a level at which it is more easily achieved.

A long apprenticeship is often required to learn all the skills demanded by the climbs in this book. Rapid changes in the weather bring rapid changes to winter climbing conditions and create almost unique styles of climbing. In this dynamic environment it can be very difficult to choose the best route to climb on any given day, especially when there are so many different types of climb to choose from.

The art of choosing the best route to climb is one that is learned through many years of trying – and often failing – to decipher the varied influences of the weather. As well as helping you to find and follow the routes, this book aims to speed up your learning of the dark arts of winter route choice and to reduce the number of failed missions.

After 27 years of winter climbing, 22 of which were spent as a full-time mountain guide, I have learned a lot about Scottish winter climbing. Building on my last edition of this book, I describe the various styles of climb, what weather conditions are required to create them, and how to choose the best climb for the forecast weather. It is a broad selection of winter climbs and every route has been categorised into one (or more) of these styles.

In this way, if the conditions favour a particular style of climb, you can find a crag that has climbs of that style and a route at a suitable grade. Once you've chosen the best route for you, the crag and route descriptions will allow you to find and follow the climb, with new photo diagrams and information about descents back to the glen.

Climbing conditions in recent years have been as variable as ever. We've had some very good winters since the last edition of this guidebook was published – and some very poor winters. Elliot's Downfall on Aonach Dubh in Glen Coe formed and was climbed in 2021 for the first time since 1996. Many other low-level cascade climbs formed, as well as some of the rare thin face climbs on Ben Nevis. In contrast, in February in 2019 it was possible to rock-climb Observatory Ridge to the summit of Ben Nevis with bare hands on dry rock. Climate change may bring more or less snow, more storms or fewer, better or worse climbing conditions; we will have to wait and see. There is likely to be change, though.

Most of us want to find good climbing on routes climbed in their 'normal' style. Green Gully, on the Comb, is normally a snow-ice climb and most people want to climb it like this and to know when the snow-ice will be good. This book will help you decide when climbs are likely to be in their optimum condition in their 'normal' style. However, the intention is not to make climbers feel restricted to climbing the routes in the style as described. Many mixed climbs were first done in icier conditions than might commonly be found now, and sharing information on which climbs work well as snowed-up rock climbs is useful. As an example, I climbed Clough's Chimney, also on the Comb, as a snowed-up rock route and decided the description of it rarely forming as a winter climb was inaccurate. It's a good snowed-up rock climb; no ice is required. If you do attempt a climb that's not in its 'normal' style, bear in mind that the grade might be very different to what it is normally.

However, there is more to winter climbing than just climbing the route. Learning how to take care of yourself in full winter conditions is still a prerequisite for anyone climbing here and is a skill as important as any climbing technique. Indeed, on some

## WINTER CLIMBING: A RECENT HISTORY

days just surviving the weather is the challenge, whether you manage any climbing or not!

Many of the routes described in this guide are longer than experienced anywhere else in British mountains and are of alpine-like seriousness. It is not a good idea to be lured onto the famous Tower Ridge of Ben Nevis for your first Scottish winter climb. The Lochaber Mountain Rescue Team has escorted dozens of shivering 'all-nighters' off this route in the dull grey hours of dawn! Try something shorter to start with as a 'wee Scottish apprenticeship'.

A combination of short daylight hours, possible strong winds and poor snow conditions add to the serious nature of Scottish winter climbing. Fitness is of prime importance to sustain climbers through long hours, carrying far more weight in their rucksacks than would be experienced in the summer months. Climbers must be economical with their time and aim to keep moving as efficiently as is practical, in order to avoid a possibly serious benightment or slip on a dark and unfamiliar descent. Records show that novice and experienced climbers alike come to grief on these Scottish mountains, sometimes with fatal consequences.

Scottish winter climbing is good sport, but don't treat these routes as 'sport climbs'!

## WINTER CLIMBING: A RECENT HISTORY

The traditional approach to climbing is strongly maintained in Scotland, with the history of the climbs being well remembered. Modern ice climbing was developed here, and that heritage adds greatly to the modern-day climbing experience.

In the winter of 1960, Scottish climbers Jimmy Marshall and Robin

*Early ice axes, including Hamish MacInnes' Terrordactyl in the centre*

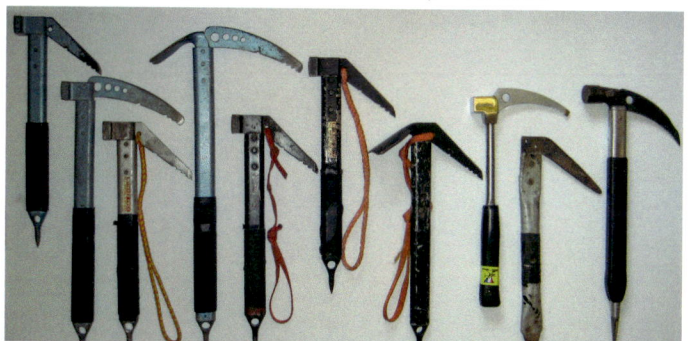

Smith completed the most significant week of climbing ever achieved in Scotland. First ascents of Orion Direct, Smith's Route and Minus Two Gully, and the first single-day and free ascent of Point Five Gully, all on Ben Nevis, were among the seven climbs they completed on consecutive days. All of this was achieved with a single ice axe each and crampons with no front points.

Ten years later, American Yvon Chouinard made a brief visit to Glen Coe which was to trigger a change that would revolutionise winter climbing. Using prototype curved ice hammers, he made some very fast ascents, demonstrating how to climb ice by direct aid, hanging off the pick itself embedded in the ice. On comparing techniques with local climbers John Cunningham, Hamish MacInnes and many others in the Clachaig Inn one night, modern ice climbing was born.

*Number Three Gully, Ben Nevis – a classic snow gully*

Also in 1970, Hamish MacInnes developed the 'Terrordactyl' – a short, all-metal ice tool with a steeply dropped pick. The 'Terror' and Chouinard's ice hammer dominated the forefront of international ice climbing for several years. Eventually these two designs were combined to create the banana pick which is still the basis for modern ice tool design. Today, 50 years on from the Terrordactyl, we are still using the same techniques.

Scottish winter climbing has always been at the forefront of global climbing standards. The world's hardest traditionally protected winter climb is currently found on Ben Nevis: Anubis, first climbed by local resident Dave MacLeod.

### Hamish MacInnes

In so many ways, Hamish MacInnes contributed more to mountain culture than anyone else in Scotland. The 'Fox of Glencoe' died in November 2020, leaving a legacy of literature and films, groundbreaking developments in climbing and mountain rescue tools and techniques, as well as world-class first ascents of climbs in various countries. Hamish had an unorthodox character and pragmatic approach to risk and loss, and enjoyed being able to help rescue people just as much as his personal mountaineering achievements. He was one of the greatest mountaineers of our time.

## HAUNT OF THE RAVEN BY HAMISH MACINNES
### (WRITTEN IN MAY 2010)

When I was asked to do a short piece for this guidebook, I thought 'what the Hell......?' . Who wants to read personal crap of what happened to someone who may have misread the guidebook or were too ambitious. Then I had second thoughts – why not? I'm sure Iain Clough would have gone for the idea - giving climb descriptions a human touch. What really evolves when you convert the written word into vertical action and all the other factors come into play? To put it another way, when the budgy hits the fan.

I am more in sympathy with two pals, John MacSnorrt and Wullie Flyte in the poem. "The Conquest of Buachaille Etive" by E. A. Balfour. John McSnorrt a rough, tough mountaineer, Wullie more gentile. Upon bagging the summit Wullie exclaimed:-

"Peak upon peak sae fair and grand,
Like elfin towers in fairyland……."
MacSnorrt said: "Dinna be sae fulish,
There's naethin' there but Ballachulish."

My brief contribution is a tale of three climbers, John Cullen, Charlie Vigano of the Creagh Dhu and myself who in the early 1950's attempted the first winter ascent of Ravens Gully on Buachaille Etive Mor; Ravens is a gash on the side of North Buttress, a prodigious prop of solid porphyry which sweeps up from the Moor of Rannoch to the very summit of the Buachaille. The gully is an annex on the right of this, wet and dripping in summer, frigid in winter when adorned with the white fangs of icicles.

'Ye can't come up here Jimmy!'. Two black angry acrobatic residents screamed at us as we roped up at the first obstacle, the overhanging Pitch 4. In those days climbing gear was scarce and the Glasgow shipyards was our source of hardware. For clothing there was the Barras where you didn't ask questions and watched your small change. The week before one piece flying suits were Lost Leaders - ex RAF, insulated and only £1.50p each. They sported numerous pockets, two of which were on the lower outer legs of the suit, excellent for an aviator's map and notebook, but useless on upside down moves on the aforementioned Pitch 4 where I did lose some loose change.

Ravens is a climb that grabs attention, where each succeeding pitch feels harder than the last. Thus engaged, the day slipped by and shadows began to crowd the defile. It was on the last pitch that the budgy, if not a raven, hit the proverbial fan. I had run out most of our 160ft. long rope when it jammed. I tried to descend but it was too dangerous and there were no belays. It was almost dark and I wasn't dressed for the occasion having only a thin ex-WD anorak over an old summer shirt. I untied and continued, soloing up steep ice, eventually coming to a halt in a short step, called the "Corkscrew," aptly named. I jammed myself in this enclave with one crampon jammed in an iced crack and my other foot on the wall on my right. It was now about 4pm and very dark, but I could shout to my two friends ensconced under the overhanging walls at the bottom of Ravens Direct Finish, then also unclimbed. This was their belay point. I envied their flying suits, which they now wore. I had left mine to be hauled up at the top of my pitch as it was too bulky to climb in as I had discovered lower down.

Fortunately we had mentioned to Bill Smith also of the Creagh Dhu where we were going.

Bill retorted:

"Well when I go down to the Clachaig Inn tonight I won't be looking up at the Buachaille for your lights."

But he did and saw John and Charlie's distress signal. Eight hours later I heard a cry from above, it was Bill with a posse of top climbers including Jimmy Marshall. I still feel a coldness in my spine when I think of that wonderful day.

*Hamish MacInnes*

## TYPES OF WINTER CLIMBS: SNOW, ICE AND MIXED

Every route in this guide is assigned a category to indicate the overall character or style of that route.
- Snow
- Ice
- Mixed

There are, of course, overlaps and crossovers, but the aim is to give you an idea of the main feel of a climb and what it takes to bring it into normal climbing condition.

### Snow

The great snow gullies of Ben Nevis and Glen Coe are obvious and alluring objectives which drew the attention of the first mountaineers. They can offer journeys through impressive rock formations on reasonable ground. They can also hold the highest avalanche hazard. Grade I snow gullies (see explanation of grades in 'Using this guide') tend to be found at an altitude and aspect that collects lots of fresh snow blown in by the typical westerly winds. They steepen to around 45 degrees and often form large cornices at their tops. This combination makes them more prone to avalanche than anywhere else. Take great care to assess the avalanche hazard in these gullies.

*Abseiling into Tower Gully, Ben Nevis, using a snow bollard*

The snow on these routes is transformed over time and especially by thaw-freeze cycles rounding off the snow crystals into individual tiny lumps of ice. Soft snow that can make upward progress nearly impossible soon after it has accumulated is turned into firm snow that supports your weight and can hold a boot print. Kicking and cutting steps in the snow like this is a time-honoured mountaineering skill that should be practised by everyone and is very rewarding.

Further transformation of the snow can make it hard and icy, demanding good crampon technique to avoid the serious consequence of a long slide down into the corrie. Climbing, and especially descending, these gullies on hard icy snow is a serious business, especially since the big gullies rarely offer many opportunities for rock or ice protection. An understanding of how to build snow anchors and how to belay to reduce shock loads onto them is essential. Snow gullies rarely turn into snow-ice, due to the depth of snow they hold, but can occasionally have icy steps in them early in the winter season when there is little snow cover.

The approaches to most of the climbs on Ben Nevis involve grade I snow slopes, so it is important that climbers become comfortable moving around on these big, serious snow slopes.

Cornices form when wind blows snow over an edge. Wind moving over the top of the edge creates low pressure which draws air up the steep ground underneath (this effect is what makes aeroplanes fly). The air going up the steep ground meets the air going over the top and creates an area of rotating air at the lip of the steep ground. Both streams of air, over the top and up the steep ground, carry snow and this is then packed into an overhanging crest of snow. Cornices can grow very quickly. In a couple of hours they can be big enough to start falling off and in a few days they can be a couple of metres wide. Cornices present major obstacles on reaching the top of a climb and when walking along the plateau near the edge.

Cornices are biggest in the centre of big gullies and smallest (or non-existent) above the ridges to each side of the gully. This is because the air being drawn up the crag is channelled into the deep gully, carrying the most snow and building the biggest cornice. Ridges separate the air stream being drawn up the crag and minimise the cornice-building effect. So, if you're faced with a big cornice above you, try to move onto the ridge at the side to reach the top. Or descend the climb! Tunnelling underneath cornices was once popular but lost its appeal a long time ago.

In one notable example, a very experienced French mountain guide triggered a cornice collapse at the top of Number Four Gully. He was standing 4m from the edge when it broke away 1m further back from the edge. A 5m depth of cornice carried him down to Lochan Coire na Ciste from where he crawled to the CIC hut with a broken leg.

## Ice

Ice climbs can be sub-categorised into the four styles below.

### Snow-ice climbs

Scotland's most common and most famous style of winter climbing is snow-ice climbing in gullies. Point Five Gully is possibly the most famous example and is known the world over. Green Gully and Comb Gully, also on Ben Nevis; Crowberry Gully on Buachaille Etive Mòr; and SC Gully on Stob Coire nan Lochan are also snow-ice climbs.

Snow-ice does not form with cold weather alone. Instead, we need snowfall and the right direction of wind to fill the gully with snow, just enough thaw to make the snow wet without melting too much away, then a good freeze to make it solid. This snow-thaw-freeze cycle needs to be repeated a few times to form sufficient snow-ice in the gully to climb. Too little thaw before the freeze will result in firm snow rather than solid snow-ice, or a surface layer of snow-ice on top of softer snow. Then we need a calm

## Types of Winter Climbs: Snow, Ice and Mixed

day with no snowfall and a freezing level below the bottom of the route for it to be in condition.

The west coast of Scotland typically benefits from lots of snowfall accompanied by strong winds and temperatures that can change by 10°C in just a few hours (and sometimes back again in the next few hours). Soft snow is transported by the wind to collect in sheltered slopes and is funnelled by gullies. It is warmed in the following thaw and becomes wet from partial melt or through rainfall. It then freezes into a more solid version of snow if there's a subsequent freeze. This is how snow-ice is formed, and its quality depends on the precise balance of volume of snow, depth and duration of thaw, rain, and how well frozen it is afterwards. With just a minor change in any one of these variables, the quality of the resulting snow-ice changes greatly.

The depth and duration of a thaw required to saturate the snow is greater than might be expected. There can be periods of thaw with heavy rain lasting four or five days so it might seem everything will have been washed away, when in fact the ice factory of Ben Nevis has turned the snow into wonderful snow-ice.

There are also other factors to consider in this balance. The depth of fresh snow accumulation is a big one. With more soft snow, a longer and deeper thaw is required to saturate the snow all the way to the bottom. A single day of thaw with rain is unlikely to penetrate through snow of more than 50cm in depth. Snow in the steeper gullies on the climbs might not be this thick and might be turned into reasonable snow-ice after a thaw of one day followed by a good freeze. The snow in the corries and big, easy gullies will be thicker (1–5m depth), and the snow on the exit slopes of climbs will be deeper and require a longer thaw to become properly saturated.

The temperature of the rocks and the ground is also a big factor. If the ground is not well frozen, a short thaw can do a lot of damage by melting away snow. If the ground is very cold and frozen hard, a thaw can make more ice form by releasing water into the cold ground where it freezes. As a very rough guide, a thaw of 24hr, especially if there's no rain, is too short to saturate the snow; 48hr with rain is often about right for snow in the gullies to become wet enough to refreeze into snow-ice; and 72hr or more of thaw can be OK if the ground was frozen hard before the thaw.

However, snow-ice rarely forms as a result of a single thaw-freeze cycle. It normally requires many such cycles to change the structure of the snow and to build the snow-ice sufficiently. The winter brings a continuous succession of snow-thaw-freeze cycles of differing lengths and depths, requiring assessment of the quality of the ice prior to every climb.

Snow-ice forms in gullies quicker than any other type of ice and it represents the most reliable style of climb.

Gullies catch snow being blown over the top and funnel it into exactly the right place. During a thaw, water is also funnelled into the gully and through the snow there, accelerating the effect of the thaw-freeze cycle. At the start of winter it takes a few snow-thaw-freeze cycles to transform the snow into solid snow-ice, even though it might look solid and good to climb beforehand. The first climbing team onto a snow-ice climb each winter always takes a bit of a gamble; there have been many occasions when I've started up a climb only to find the good-looking ice is actually firm snow that's terrifying to climb. With subsequent thaw-freeze cycles and more snowfall, these climbs build and become more solid and secure to climb.

By the end of the winter the snow-ice can transform all the way to something close to cascade ice, but this takes months and many storms to achieve. Snow-ice can form as early as December and last as late as May.

At its best, snow-ice can offer the perfect combination of 'plastic', dependable ice that does not shatter when you place a pick but is sufficiently solid to place good ice screws into. The 'honeycomb' structure provided by millions of tiny air-pockets in the snow creates a texture that absorbs the strike of a pick instead of shattering like cascade ice. At its worst, a snow-ice climb can be vertical snow that is too soft to hold an ice axe, let alone an ice screw.

See the picture of Point Five Gully, Ben Nevis, on page 6 of the Ben Nevis volume for an example of a snow-ice climb.

### Thin face ice climbs

Snow-ice forms very readily in gullies due to the funnel effect of the gully. Snow-ice also forms on open cliffs, although it is a much slower process. If the snow is wet and sticky as it falls, and if rime ice grows on the rocks as well, ice will form on the open faces more readily. After a whole winter of snow-thaw-freeze cycles the snow-ice on some very open faces can form into thin ice routes. These are highly sought-after and typical of Scottish ice climbing; thin, bold, exposed and brilliant.

In a good winter a plating of snow-ice slowly forms over all the rocks. The character of these climbs is of ice climbing on an open face where you would not expect to find ice at all. The exposure and tenuous nature of the ice make for a rewarding and memorable experience. The skill comes in following the thicker lines of ice up the cliff and avoiding the lines that peter out into nothing despite it all looking much the same.

Ben Nevis is the home of the thin face ice climb. Indicator Wall, immediately below the summit, holds most of the real classics such as Psychedelic Wall, Albatross, Riders on the Storm and Ship of Fools. Mega classic routes such as Orion Direct and Astral Highway are similar to this category

*Climbing thin face ice on the Second Slab Rib, The Long Climb Finish to Orion Direct*

but their formation is aided by slight dribbles of water that flow down their lines. Others on Orion Face, such as Journey into Space and Space Walk, are true thin face ice routes that require a long winter of storms and thaw-freeze cycles, and are highly sought-after climbs due to their rare occurrence and memorable nature.

Do not expect thin face ice climbs to be formed before late February, but they can remain in place until late in the spring. Easter used to be the traditional period for ice climbing, and it is still the case that April can be the best time for thin face ice climbing.

### Cascade ice climbs

Elsewhere in the world, ice climbing is usually cascade ice climbing. Waterfalls freeze in persistent cold temperatures to form cascades of pure, hard ice. A steady source of water and reliably cold weather without too much precipitation create ideal conditions for forming this kind of ice. In Scotland we do occasionally experience such conditions, but they rarely stay with us for more than a couple of weeks. Here, when cascade ice climbs form they quickly become very popular as everyone rushes to climb them before they melt away again.

Cascade ice is dense and forms beautiful shapes and features. The colder it is, the denser it is. Its density demands sharp picks and ice screws, and an accurate swing with an ice axe. The shapes and features often help by providing useful places for hooking and placing front points. The density of this ice also makes it quite durable in a thaw. It doesn't melt straight away; it can survive a thaw. However, cascade ice can become detached from the rock behind it and can fall apart in blocks when it does melt. It is best to avoid cascade ice in a thaw and be careful after a thaw once it has refrozen, to make sure it's securely held in place. Sunshine in the spring can also create unpleasant conditions in cascade ice due to the partial warming of the ice by solar radiation.

Blue Riband in Glen Coe, Steall Falls in Glen Nevis, most of the climbs at Beinn Udlaidh and Eilde Canyon are cascade ice climbs. After a week or more of temperatures around -10°C at sea level these climbs might have formed well enough to attempt. Take sharp picks and crampons, and lots of ice screws.

**Snow patch cascade ice climbs**
Even more rarely, the balance of thaw and refreeze is such that a unique type of ice cascade can form. In their style of climbing, these are very similar to cascade climbs, but instead of the water supply coming from a stream or a spring, the water is supplied by the snow patch above the climb. Once snow has built up, a thaw will allow water to run down the climb. A hard freeze will then start to form cascade-style ice below the snow patch.

Mega Route X is a great example of this type of climb which requires a very specific combination of lots of snow, deep thaws and hard freezes to form. Consequently, it forms very rarely and is highly prized when it does. Mega Route X will not form in a prolonged period of freezing conditions in the way that Blue Riband will, or the climbs at Beinn Udlaidh. Look out for rapid (24hr) periods of thaw with rain when the snow cover is good already, and subsequent hard refreezes.

**Variations and combinations**
Many climbs fall neatly into one of the above categories, but there are also many that are a mixture of two or three styles of climb. Hadrian's Wall Direct on Ben Nevis is a snow-ice

*The author climbing cascade ice on Gemini, Ben Nevis*

*Climbing snow patch cascade ice on Mega Route X, Ben Nevis*

## THE NATURAL ORDER OF ICE CLIMBS

Of the cascade ice climbs, routes at Beinn Udlaidh form quite quickly. Waterfall Gully and Compression Cracks on Ben Nevis might form soon after, and climbs such as Blue Riband, Finnisg-aig Falls and Steall Falls require a long time of very cold weather.

As you walk up Allt a' Mhuilinn you might see ice forming in Waterfall Gully on the side of Carn Dearg Buttress. This is a good sign that it's been cold enough and that there'll be good ice elsewhere. The Carn Dearg Cascades close to the CIC hut are at a similar altitude to the climbs at Beinn Udlaidh and are the same type of cascade climbs. So if there's good ice here, the climbs at Beinn Udlaidh will be good.

Ice often forms early on in Coire Leis. It's a long walk up to the Little Brenva Face, and you can't see the face to assess it until high in the corrie, but Final Buttress and Bob Run are very reliable early-season climbs. If there's ice in Waterfall Gully, there'll be some ice on the Little Brenva Face.

Snow-ice climbs require a succession of snow-thaw-freeze cycles generated by storms and fluctuating temperatures. Number Three Gully Buttress on Ben Nevis has a pitch of snow-ice at the start which is one of the first snow-ice climbs to form each winter. It's located at a high altitude and funnels water running down from above in a groove where lots of snow collects – a happy combination for creating snow-ice. This is a good early-season ice climb with rocky mixed climbing in the second half of the route. Number Three Gully Buttress is a good early-season ice climb with rocky mixed climbing in the second half of the route. Soon afterwards, Green Gully and Comb Gully are likely to hold enough snow-ice. The first pitch of Green Gully can be quite soft (firm snow rather than solid snow-ice) for a while even though it looks good, but higher up the gully the ice is usually better.

Glover's Chimney and The White Line, South, Central, Central Right Hand and North Gullies on Creag Coire na Ciste form up next, along with Left Twin and Right Twin on Aonach Mòr. Tower Scoop and Gardyloo Gully can be good places to find fun ice climbing from early February. All of these are at around 1100m altitude and east facing so they collect lots of snow. Point Five Gully, Hadrian's Wall Direct and Zero Gully will be next to form, along with Smith's Route and Indicator Wall. Orion Direct and the Minus Gullies take longer still because they have less of a funnel effect to collect dribbles of water, so they require more thaw-freeze cycles to form.

Crowberry Gully on Buachaille Etive Mòr and SC Gully on Stob Coire nan Lochan are lower down and require generally colder weather to form snow-ice compared with the higher climbs on Ben Nevis. This is the same for The Curtain on Ben Nevis, which is an obvious route and very popular once it's iced up. If The Curtain is formed, Crowberry Gully and SC Gully are likely to be formed as well.

climb that also has a notable spring at the top which dribbles water down the line, helping the ice to form. There is a slight funnel effect on the face, similar to a gully, that directs the snow tumbling down the face. In a thaw, dribbles of water will naturally run down the snow on the climb, aiding the formation of snow-ice. So, it's a thin face climb that forms in a similar way to snow-ice climbs with the benefit of having a spring at the top, which itself can produce cascade-style ice. Hence, it forms readily and is one of the most reliable grade V snow-ice climbs.

The Curtain, also on Ben Nevis, lies underneath a funnel that pours snow down onto the climb. There's also a small spring that dribbles water down the route. In very cold weather with no snow there's a formation of cascade ice on the route due to the spring, but this is unlikely to form fully. Snowfall and a couple of thaw-freeze cycles are also required to form the climb properly. So, this is a snow-ice climb that continues to transform into what feels like a cascade climb quite quickly.

On some climbs there are whole pitches of one style followed by further pitches of a different style. Compression Crack on Ben Nevis is a good example; it has cascade ice in the first couple of pitches followed by steep snow-ice to finish. It's common to find the cascade ice fully formed but the upper pitches of snow-ice not formed at all due to the different weather required to form the different styles of ice.

## Mixed climbing

Mixed climbs can be sub-categorised into the four styles below.

### General mixed climbs

Mixed climbs feature a combination of rock, ice and turf in varying degrees. In this book, mixed climbs that include all of these, and do not have a strong characteristic towards any one of those components, will be referred to simply as general mixed climbs.

Mixed climbing has always been pursued in Scotland, but it has become more popular and more refined in the last couple of decades. It started out with the great ridges and buttresses such as Tower Ridge on Ben Nevis and Curved Ridge on Buachaille Etive Mòr – obvious mountaineering objectives that drew the attention of the first climbers exploring these mountains.

Tower Ridge is a mixed climb, requiring movement over rock, snow, ice and occasional patches of frozen turf. The relative quantities of each of these depends on the conditions at the time. Early in winter, Tower Ridge can have a thin coating of snow and rime, and verglas (a thin covering of transparent ice) on the rocks, demanding the use of crampons even though you are essentially climbing the rocks. In the depths of the winter there can be so much snow cover that the ridge is climbed mostly on hard, crispy snow with occasional touches of rock at the hardest sections. Later in the spring, rock handholds melt out of the snow but hard, icy snow remains under the feet, making progress simple and particularly enjoyable, especially in the April sunshine.

Modern mixed climbing has diversified and specialised in the same way that all aspects of climbing have evolved. For a while, there was a focus on climbing classic rock climbs in winter – a trend that met with some resistance due to the concerns over damage done to the rock. This is still a concern, and if attempting to climb highly regarded rock climbs it's important to climb in a way that leaves no permanent marks on the rocks.

Currently, there is a drive to find 'winter-only' climbs. These are routes that will not be fun in the summer due to vegetation, green rocks, lines of seepage and loose ground that is frozen solid in winter but dangerous to climb in the summer.

Whereas in ice climbing there is a limit to the level of difficulty due to the nature of how ice forms, in mixed climbing there is virtually no limit. The hardest ice climb in Scotland is (probably) Jane's Weep (VIII,8) on Aonach Dubh in Glen Coe. What is possibly the hardest naturally protected winter climb in the world is found on Ben Nevis: Anubis, climbed by Dave MacLeod in 2010 and repeated twice since. Greg Boswell McInnes made the third ascent in 2018 – a particularly poor winter for climbing. Anubis might be around grade XIII – some five grades harder than Jane's Weep. This illustrates the attraction of mixed climbing; good climbing conditions can form quickly and there is ample opportunity for a challenging climb.

In the same way as with ice climbing, judging the nature of the climbing conditions is a tricky job and one that demands dedication, time and many attempts, likely both successful and unsuccessful. Once you know what to look for and how the recent weather affects the climbs, you'll be able to make better decisions.

Mixed climbs need to be white and frozen to be in acceptable condition. By consensus that has been reached over many decades, and due to the unnecessary damage it can cause, dry tooling is not considered acceptable on Scottish crags away from some low-level training crags. In the mountains, the crag needs to be wintry in appearance, white with snow or rime, and frozen. This is the ethical approach that has developed over many years and is peculiar to Scotland. Many foreign climbers are baffled by these restrictions, but we abide by them to maintain the quality of experience and so that we are all playing by the same rules. Rime and snow on the rocks does not protect the rocks to any significant extent; climbing black rocks is cheating! Waiting until the crag is properly frozen protects turf from excessive damage, and the blocks are more likely to be frozen and held in place.

### Rocky mixed climbs

Rocky mixed climbs (or snowed-up rock climbs) can be the first to freeze due to being made up of solid rock. Even so, blocks, chockstones and flakes need to be frozen in place, and this takes a couple of weeks of sub-zero conditions at the start of winter. They often make a good choice for the first climbs of the winter season because they're early to freeze, don't require any thaw-freeze cycles and can offer reasonable protection. Even so, a thaw and refreeze can provide the snow-ice required to hold blocks and chockstones in place. They can be a bit rattly before this happens.

'Snowed-up rock climb' is actually an unhelpful name for this style of climb. It is rime that is more effective at making the climb white and that will provide better climbing conditions. Rime is a type of ice crystal that grows on any surface exposed to humid air being blown onto it in a

## TYPES OF WINTER CLIMBS: SNOW, ICE AND MIXED

sub-zero temperature. It is often seen on fence posts and, perhaps confusingly, grows into the wind. So, you need a wind blowing cloud onto the crag and the temperature to be below zero. No snowfall is required at all. After a westerly gale, choose a crag that faces west and has been in the cloud.

The best conditions in which I've climbed snowed-up rock have included well-frozen rocks and a light rime of a couple of centimetres that is easily brushed away to reveal (hopefully) cracks and ledges underneath. The crags have been totally white at the start of the day, with the climbs brushed free of rime by climbers on various routes.

Sufficient rime to make crags and climbs white enough to climb can form overnight. Twelve hours of strong winds blowing freezing clouds onto the crag is enough to form a couple of centimetres of rime over every surface of the crag.

Delicate dry rime can fall off the crag in a strong wind and is likely to fall off in very dry, cold air. This means that the crag can be white one day and black the next despite the temperature staying below zero. Once the crag is out of the cloud the rime will start to deteriorate. Sunshine will also strip rime from the rocks faster than you can climb them.

Over time, rime can grow to be a metre deep, and it turns very icy

*Donald King making the first ascent of Engineers Cracks, Buachaille Etive Mòr, in perfect conditions for rocky mixed climbing*

*Hoar frost crystals that've grown on cold, still nights with a hard frost*

after thaw-freeze cycles. In March, the summit observatory ruins on Ben Nevis are often covered by incredibly thick rime ice that has built up over the previous three or four months and survived many thaw-freeze cycles. This type of rime makes life difficult if you want to climb the rock underneath it. In thick, icy rime it can be a monumental struggle to clear the rime off the rocks for a whole pitch.

Hoar frost is very different to rime, apart from being a type of ice crystal. Hoar frost forms during a cold, still, starlit night and is what glistens on the grass and in the trees after a hard frost. Crystals of ice grow upwards as moisture in the air falls onto horizontal surfaces. Since hoar frost only forms on horizontal surfaces, it doesn't turn steep crags white. So, by itself, it is not sufficient to create the winter conditions required.

Thaw-freeze cycles create dribbles of water that run into cracks and refreeze. Iced-up cracks are a problem; finding pick placements can be very difficult and uncovering protection incredibly tiring. Snowed-up rock climbs are best early in the season when the cracks are still clear of ice and the rime is light and fluffy.

Snowfall can also make a crag white in appearance. Cold, dry snow will not stick to the rocks; it'll pile up on ledges, making the crag look white from above but not from below. However, if the snow is a bit wet (this happens when the temperature is at or not far below freezing) it can stick to the rocks and make the whole crag go white. This wet snow can also freeze into an unhelpful icy crust which is hard to clear from the rocks when you're climbing.

## Types of winter climbs: snow, ice and mixed

Some snow on the ledges is very often helpful on all mixed climbs, especially if it has transformed to snow-ice after thaw-freeze cycles and provides ice axe placements to pull on, and a more secure surface to stand on with crampons.

Curved Ridge on Buachaille Etive Mòr, Crest Route on Stob Coire nan Lochan, and Slab Climb and Gargoyle Wall on Ben Nevis are all excellent snowed-up rock climbs.

### Turfy mixed climbs

Turf freezes slowly. Small tufts of turf freeze first, and freeze most quickly when they're exposed to a cold wind. Wind chill affects the crag in the same way as it affects us when we're exposed to the wind. Big patches of turf can take many weeks to freeze properly but can be damaged or even completely removed from the crag if they're climbed over before they're frozen. Turf in chimneys, corners and gullies that do not experience the chilling effect of the wind takes longer to freeze.

Turf normally takes two to three weeks of sub-zero, windy conditions to freeze properly, and even then it benefits from a couple of snow-thaw-freeze cycles to consolidate properly. If the turf is very dry it will not be good to climb on, even if it's frozen. It becomes very crumbly and easy to break up if it's too dry. Wet turf freezes into a much more solid medium. Turf can be wet from rain that fell before the freeze, or it can be made wet by

*Climbing Turf War, a turfy mixed climb on Douglas Boulder, Ben Nevis*

thaw-freeze cycles with rain or drainage in the cliff running onto the turf.

In any case, turf must be frozen to climb. Since it is difficult to assess the quality of the turf at the start of the winter without climbing on it, it's worth waiting a week or two longer to make sure. Don't head out at the first sign of snow or rime.

However, once properly frozen, turf will stay frozen through some quite substantial periods of thaw. It will hold water in a thaw which will dribble down below the turf and freeze into ice of one sort or another in the refreeze. So, turfy mixed climbs can become really quite icy over the course of the winter. There's nothing more satisfying than placing a pick in a solid, icy lump of turf!

Turf commonly holds snow on top of it, and this is transformed into snow-ice with thaw-freeze cycles. So, turfy mixed climbs quite often turn into true mixed climbs over the course of a good winter, with a mixture of turf, rock, ice and snow-ice.

Turfy mixed climbs, like any mixed climbs, should look wintry and white. Rime and snow should cover the rocks. There's an argument that only the turf needs to be frozen and icy, that the rocks don't need to be white as well since they're not used for climbing. This is mostly the case on sandstone and quartzite crags found in the far north-west, and is also a matter of opinion. It might be easier to say that all mixed climbs should be white and wintry in appearance with the rocks covered in rime or snow.

### Icy mixed climbs

Mixed climbs are found on buttresses and ridges and therefore don't normally form very much ice. However, some mixed climbs benefit from or rely on a certain amount of ice. The ice is normally snow-ice that requires snow to collect on the route followed by a thaw-freeze cycle to saturate the snow and turn it into ice.

Raeburn's Arête and Tower Face of The Comb on Ben Nevis are good examples. Wet snow sticks to the rocks readily when the temperature is close to freezing at the right altitude. If this snowfall is followed by a thaw-freeze cycle, the snow will turn into sufficiently solid snow-ice to make the climb viable. Without this covering of snow-ice, the slabs will be very difficult to climb.

The Great Ridge of Garbh Bheinn is another example. The lower pitches of the direct start follow turf and rock ramps, ideally covered in solid snow. With this combination the climbing is great fun and relatively straightforward. Without it, you'll be climbing steep turf and rock slabs with soft useless snow covering anything useful. Judging when the snow has transformed into snow-ice in the right places is difficult.

Thompson's Route on Ben Nevis is usually a mixed climb that normally requires snow-ice. I climbed it once without ice on the first pitch

## Types of winter climbs: snow, ice and mixed

and found it was much harder than normal. A good amount of ice needs to build up in the initial chimney to make the grade IV climbing you'd expect. Thompson's Route follows a chimney that catches plenty of snow which transforms into good snow-ice so that, late in the season, it can build so much ice that it's climbed entirely on ice and feels like an ice climb.

### Combinations and variations

Mixed climbs have a combination of rock, ice and turf with varying amounts of each of these ingredients. For climbs that particularly rely on one or more of these ingredients, this book uses the subcategories of turfy mixed climb, icy mixed climb and rocky mixed climb to highlight that you want to have good conditions for these elements.

For example, Crest Route is a rocky mixed climb, so it will be good to climb when the rocks are rimed and frozen. It does not rely on frozen turf or ice. However, Raeburn's Route is a turfy and icy mixed climb, so you should wait until the turf is well frozen and a couple of thaw-freeze cycles have produced some snow-ice on the route. Chimney Route relies on the turf being well frozen, having some ice in the chimney and the rocks being rimed up, so all three categories are mentioned. Mixed climbing conditions need to be very good for this to be a good option.

Some other climbs change character during the course of the winter. For example, Taliballan on Stob Coire an Laoigh is a wonderful turfy mixed climb early in the winter that turns into a brilliant icy mixed climb with varying amounts of turf and snow-ice depending on the nature of the winter storms. So, Taliballan is categorised as a turfy mixed OR icy mixed climb.

*Climbing Lost The Place, an icy mixed climb on Ben Nevis*

## Winter Climbs: Glen Coe

Lost the Place on Ben Nevis can require hooking on snowed-up rock in the final chimney, or it can be climbed with a lot of ice in the chimney and over the final chockstone. With picks in the ice, front points on rock while back-and-footing up the chimney you can really appreciate all the techniques of winter climbing. In this book I have described it as a rocky mixed OR icy mixed climb.

In the same way, Morwind is a very good turfy mixed climb on Aonach Mòr which changes in character to an icy mixed climb and can actually form so much snow-ice that you don't need to use the rock at all.

### WEATHER

The west coast of Scotland receives a wide variety of ever-changing weather. It is located very far north; Glasgow is at about the same latitude as Moscow and Copenhagen – much further north than Calgary and Cogne – but has a much more temperate climate due to the proximity of the Atlantic Ocean and the Gulf Stream bringing warm water to the coastline. It is located close to the polar front jet stream which moves around and often travels from the north of the UK to the south or vice versa. This shift has a huge impact on the type of weather experienced. The prevailing weather comes

*Looking down Glen Coe from Stob Dearg, Buachaille Etive Mòr*

from the west and reflects where it came from: relatively warm and wet weather from a warm and wet ocean. When it's cold enough for snow in the winter there can be a lot of it, and it's always accompanied by wind.

## Wind

Possibly the biggest influence on the choice of where to go and what to climb is the wind. Very often, the wind is about 20–40mph on the tops, and finding a crag that's sheltered from the wind seems like a good idea. However, this might not always be the case. This wind speed is most effective for transportation of snow and deposition on the sheltered side of the mountain. The avalanche hazard is normally greatest in these sheltered spots, and spindrift is a major problem in all of the funnel-shaped gullies as well as approach slopes and exits to many climbs.

The wind-chill effect acts on the ground in the same way as it does on us, so a crag that's exposed to the wind will be colder and better frozen than a sheltered crag. Also, rime ice grows into the wind. You need a wind blowing cloud onto the crag and the temperature to be below zero for rime to form and to make the rocks turn white.

So, a crag that's exposed to the wind will be colder and better frozen, rimed up and blown clear of soft snow, with the least avalanche hazard and spindrift. It might be worth choosing to cope with the wind for some better climbing conditions, rather than trying to stay sheltered from it. In the depths of winter when everything is well frozen and the snow is stable, finding shelter is a good plan. At the start of the winter when the ground is still in the process of cooling down, a windward-facing crag is often a good choice.

Having said all this, when the wind is blowing spindrift up a climb and into your face as you try to see your next foot holds, things can become uncomfortable.

## Temperature

Currently, there's free access to two very detailed weather forecast sites that give accurate predictions of the temperature at summit level: Mountain Weather Information Service and the Met Office. In addition, there's real-time data from weather stations at 650m, 900m and 1200m on Aonach Mòr.

There are two measurements of temperature that are useful to know. One is the normal, 'dry-bulb' temperature. The other is the 'wet-bulb' temperature: this is measured with the mercury bulb of a classic thermometer held in a wet sponge and it normally reads a lower temperature than the dry-bulb thermometer. This is due to evaporation of water from the sponge cooling down the mercury in the bulb.

In a very dry atmosphere there's a lot of evaporation and the wet-bulb temperature is much lower than the

*About to launch up the crux of West Chimney Route on Bidean nam Bian, Glen Coe*

dry-bulb temperature. In fact, there can be spring days when the temperature is +4°C but the wet-bulb temperature is -3°C, so it feels relatively warm (due to solar radiation) but the snow and ice remain dry and frozen. Big high-pressure systems can bring these conditions with very dry, cold air and light winds. There are often hard frosts in the glens after all the cold air sinks into them overnight, with a temperature inversion making it much warmer on the tops.

When you're above the normal, dry-bulb freezing level, fresh snow is dry and it's much easier to stay warm and comfortable. You can find wet and dry temperature readings from 900m on Aonach Mòr online.

For snow-ice to form, thaw-freeze cycles are required after snowfall. A short thaw after a lot of snowfall will not make the snow wet all the way through. Only the surface layer will get soggy, so only this layer will refreeze into snow-ice, creating a crust on top of soft snow. Rain accelerates the process by saturating the snow, making it ready to refreeze into snow-ice quickly, but also by melting the snow more quickly. A thaw with no rain takes much longer to create solid snow-ice. More often, the resulting snow is firm and dry, which can be good snow to climb but is not solid enough for ice screws. Too much thaw will melt away too much snow before the refreeze. It's all in the balance of volume of snow fall, duration and depth of thaw, and speed of refreeze.

It's hard to give any guide as to how much snowfall, thaw and refreeze is required to create the perfect texture of snow-ice. If the ground is very well frozen before the thaw, the thaw will do less damage since turf and rocks warm up much more slowly than snow. Also, cascade ice thaws and melts much more slowly than snow-ice, but it does become detached from the rock. At the start of the winter, with less snow in place, a relatively short thaw will strip away too much snow. Before the ground is properly frozen the snow will melt away more quickly than it will after the ground is well frozen. It takes three weeks of sub-zero temperatures and little snow on the ground to freeze the ground properly.

Towards the end of the winter with a deep snowpack in place, it's surprising how many days of steady rain on the summit the snow can survive, especially if the ground underneath is well frozen.

Several rapid thaw-freeze cycles are better than one deep cycle, but each cycle will probably bring more snowfall which will then need to thaw and refreeze as well. There may be many occasions when you walk up thinking there'll be nothing left, only to find some brilliant ice climbing.

## Snow

With the Mountain Weather Information Service and the Met Office we're blessed with excellent weather forecasts that tell us when it will snow. The Scottish Avalanche

*Glen Coe from Stob Coire nan Lochan*

Information Service (SAIS) gives more detailed forecasts for the six areas indicated on its avalanche forecasts, including Glen Coe and Lochaber.

Snowfall by itself can make crags turn white and bring them into acceptable winter condition for mixed climbing. The snow needs to be sticky to stay on steep walls, so it needs to be around freezing. This can result in a layer of crusty snow covering the rocks, white and acceptable for mixed climbing but sometimes difficult to clear away to find cracks and ledges in the rock underneath. If it's colder, the snow will be dry and it'll simply bounce off the rocks and fall to the ground. Cold, dry snow will land on ledges but this is insufficient to make the crag turn white.

More often when it's snowing, the crags are in the cloud and rime forms on the rocks at the same time as the snow is blown onto the rocks. The white layer is then a combination of rime and snow which can get quite thick, creating a crusty, icy layer that grows to be tens of centimetres thick and is particularly difficult to climb.

**Stages of winter and their climbing styles**

October and November often bring the first falls of snow. It's an exciting time, seeing the tops of the mountains dusted with white above deep autumn colours in the glen, and anticipating the winter to come. It takes a few weeks for the ground to freeze properly, so a little patience is required before you put your training into action.

Snowed-up rock climbs are the first to come into condition – especially those with solid rock. Choose a high-level crag that faces the wind since these will freeze up first. If the crag has been in the cloud there'll be rime on the rocks facing the wind. Snowed-up rock climbs are particularly good before the first thaw-freeze cycles have dribbled water into the cracks where it freezes.

December can see the volume of snow building up and sometimes yields a long cold period. After a very cold couple of weeks, go cascade climbing. Not much snow (if any at all) is needed for these cascades to freeze up into solid, brittle ice climbs. Snowed-up rock climbs and turfy mixed climbs can be good but there is often not very much snow on the big ridges to fill in the gaps around the rocks, making them quite arduous to climb.

January is often cold, dark and stormy. Ideally, this is when there's lots of snow building up and consolidating in the thaw-freeze cycles. Stormy weather is needed to pack snow into the gullies and corries, as well as fluctuating temperatures to make the snow soggy then refreeze it into solid snow-ice. Rapidly changing conditions, short days and unsettled weather can make January a bit of a battle. With luck there'll be some mixed climbing of all types, including the rarely forming ice and mixed climbs such as Gemini, and some snow-ice climbs starting to shape up nicely.

At this time the big ridges might be covered in snow but the rocks might not be well covered, so the climbing could be somewhat slow going. These are Tower Ridge, Castle Ridge, Ledge Route, North East Buttress and Observatory Ridge on Ben Nevis; Aonach Eagach in Glen Coe, North East Ridge of Aonach Beag and Great Ridge of Garbh Bheinn. With just a little snow, these ridges are slow and painstaking climbs. Once more snow has blown onto these ridges, the gaps between the rocks get filled with snow that will then thaw and refreeze into solid snow-ice. Eventually, the rocks can become totally covered in snow and progress can become easier than

## USEFUL RESOURCES

- Mountain Weather Information Service – www.mwis.org.uk/forecasts/scottish/west-highlands
- Met Office – www.metoffice.gov.uk/weather/specialist-forecasts/mountain/southwest-highlands
- Scottish Avalanche Information Service – www.sais.gov.uk
- Weather data from Aonach Mòr at 1200m – https://holfuy.com/en/weather/1365
- Weather data from Aonach Mòr at 900m – https://holfuy.com/en/weather/195
- Weather data from Aonach Mòr at 650m – https://holfuy.com/en/weather/296
- Weather data from Glencoe Mountain (Meall a' Bhùiridh) at 360m, 750m and 1100m – www.glencoemountain.co.uk/weather
- Webcam images and weather data from CIC Hut, Ben Nevis – www.smc.org.uk/cicwebcam/cic_weather.php

*Avalanche debris in Great Gully, Buachaille Etive Mòr*

in summer. Finding anchors can of course be much harder, though.

February and March are the most reliable months of the winter. If you only have two weeks to spend climbing, go for the last week of February and the first week of March. The snow cover should have built up sufficiently to cover the rocks on approach slopes and smooth over the rocky steps on the ridges. Snow-ice should be in place in the gullies and true mixed climbs might form up. Given the right mix of thaw and refreeze, we might even see some snow patch cascades forming. So, a wide selection of climbs could be on offer.

By the end of March and into April, snow-ice might be forming on the thin face routes. As the first signs of spring appear in the glen, the high crags are still in deep winter conditions and enough storms have gone through to build a lot of ice in all the right places. If summit temperatures remain low, there's the possibility of enjoying some superb days with lots of daylight, more settled weather and good ice. The ridges will be well covered with snow, making progress easier, especially if the protection and hand holds start to appear after some sunny days. Mixed climbs are not often rimed up, so look for snow-ice climbs and thin face routes.

Very occasionally there's thin face climbing on the highest crags of Ben Nevis in May, when it's also possible to go rock climbing in warm sunshine in the glen and the big ridges feel like classic Alpine routes.

## AVALANCHES

Avalanches occur every year in Scotland, often with tragic results. In the vast majority of avalanche accidents, the avalanche is triggered by either the victim or by someone else in the victim's party. Therefore, a basic understanding of avalanches and how to avoid them should be viewed as necessary for anyone intending to climb or walk in the Scottish mountains in winter. Put simply, the ability to judge the likelihood and consequences of an avalanche, as well as what to do in the event of an avalanche incident, can save lives. There are some excellent books on the subject, with *A Chance in a Million?* by Barton and Wright being the classic text on avalanches in Scotland, and *Staying Alive in Avalanche Terrain* (3rd edition) by Bruce Tremper being an excellent more general text.

In Scotland, the highly variable winter weather tends to build up a highly layered mountain snowpack, with windblown snow accumulating as wind slab in sheltered areas. (Cracking and blocking of the snow under your feet is one way to recognise wind slab.) Avalanches can release on slopes of between about 20 and 60 degrees, with slopes of

*Cracks and blocks in the snow – an indicator of wind slab*

## MOUNTAIN RESCUE

*Lochaber Mountain Rescue Team*

Mountain rescue teams are made up of experienced and skilful local mountaineers who undergo regular training in mountaineering and remote-care first-aid skills. Rescues are coordinated by the police. These days most people carry mobile phones, and this will usually be the fastest way to contact the emergency services – assuming a signal can be found and the battery doesn't die in the cold.

If a rescue is required, call 999 and ask for police, then ask for mountain rescue.

It's worth noting that if your own mobile phone network doesn't have a signal in your location, you should try calling 999 anyway because any other network will carry the call. If this is the case, the police/mountain rescue can't call you back to follow up, so be very sure to convey detailed info about the incident. If it's not possible to make a call, attract help by shouting, by whistle or by torchlight. Personal locator beacons that work on the satellite network (not on the mobile phone network) are also available. There's also the emergencySMS (eSMS) service, which might work even if you don't have a good enough signal to make a call. You'll need to register your mobile phone before using this service by texting 'register' to 999 then following the instructions sent. In an emergency, contact the eSMS service by texting 999. Your message should include 'Police' + details of incident + location.

between about 30 and 45 degrees being the most likely to release. Above 60 degrees, the snow tends to slide off in small sluffs rather than building up to reach dangerous quantities.

The greatest danger of both avalanches and cornice collapse usually exists approximately 24 hours after a period of heavy snowfall (external loading), or during periods of thaw, especially if this is accompanied by rainfall. This danger period associated with new snow will be longer in cold temperatures when the snow will consolidate more slowly. However, cold temperatures will consolidate a wet snowpack. Even in the absence of snowfall or thaw, a significant avalanche hazard may be created by the wind re-depositing the snowpack.

Additionally, hoar frost crystals, described above, are beautiful but very dangerous when they form on the surface of the snow and are subsequently buried by further snow accumulation. They form a weak layer in the snowpack that can persist for many weeks and create a substantial avalanche hazard.

### SAIS avalanche forecasts

The Scottish Avalanche Information Service is an invaluable source of up-to-date information. From mid December until mid April, daily hazard reports and forecasts are produced for Lochaber and Glen Coe as well as four other regions, available at www.sais.gov.uk. The website also includes daily blogs by the forecasters, which can be a great source of information for assessing climbing conditions.

The avalanche forecast consists of a report on the observed conditions on the current day, and a forecast for the following day. However, it should be remembered that the forecast for the following day is dependent on the weather forecast. Mountain weather is very complex and difficult to forecast; if the weather forecast is not accurate, then the avalanche forecast may be inaccurate. The forecasts are meant as a guide and do not absolve climbers of the responsibility to make their own decisions and assessment of the avalanche hazard.

The Be Avalanche Aware (BAA) guidelines (http://beaware.sais.gov.uk) have been developed by the SAIS as a platform to encourage sensible behaviour regarding avalanches. There's also a free BAA app which can be downloaded onto mobile phones; it has various tools to help encourage safe travel and links to the SAIS forecasts.

## ACCESS

The Land Reform (Scotland) Act 2003 established statutory rights of responsible access to land and inland water for outdoor recreation and crossing land. The Scottish Outdoor Access Code (available at www.nature.scot) gives detailed guidance on the responsibilities of those exercising access rights and of those managing land and water. The Code defines how access rights should be exercised.

The three principles for responsible access apply to both the public and land managers:

- **Respect the interests of other people:** Be considerate, respect privacy and livelihoods, and the needs of those enjoying the outdoors.
- **Care for the environment:** Look after the places you visit and enjoy. Care for wildlife and historic sites.
- **Take responsibility for your own actions:** The outdoors can't be made risk-free for people exercising access rights; land managers should act with care for people's safety.

Anyone has the right to access all the climbs in this book, as long as they do so responsibly. That responsibility extends to the impact we have on the land and on the landowner's management of it, as well as the responsibility we have towards ourselves to make sure we have the skills, equipment and experience required.

## EQUIPMENT

### Map, compass and GPS

This guidebook will help climbers to find the route. It must be used in conjunction with a weather-proof map. Most of the areas in this guide are covered by OS Landranger Sheet 41: *Ben Nevis, Fort William and Glen Coe* at 1:50,000. Also, Harvey Superwalker maps for Ben Nevis and Glen Coe are easy-to-read, detailed maps at a scale of 1:25,000, and the *Ben Nevis* sheet has a superb inset of the Nevis plateau at a scale of 1:12,500. The ability to use these maps with a compass is of prime importance for all winter mountaineers and climbers.

A GPS system can provide a useful backup to more traditional map and compass skills, and it's

*The right clothing and equipment are required for extreme conditions*

recommended it is used in this way rather than using the GPS alone. Walking on the bearing obtained from a traditional compass will nearly always be steadier than following that from its satellite-driven GPS cousin. It's recommended that the GPS coordinates given in this guide are tested on a clear day and also marked on a map. This is particularly important on Ben Nevis, which is a mountain that will be revisited many times by climbers. At the foot of any steep cliff, treat all GPS readings with a great deal of caution. The cliffs can prevent accurate/strong signals from the satellites.

### Ice axes, crampons, boots, helmet

Ice axes and crampons are essential for any winter outing, whether walking or climbing. For climbing it's assumed that two tools are used. Climbing with leashless tools is now the norm at all grades – in particular for the higher grades – and lanyards connecting your tools to your harness are recommended. Stiff, waterproof and insulated boots are best for winter climbing, and when linked to a pair of clip-on crampons they provide a solid and positive base for the necessary footwork involved in climbing snow and ice. A climbing helmet is essential.

## RAVENS

*Raven on Buachaille Etive Mòr*

Ravens are remarkably intelligent birds. On Buachaille Etive Mòr they've learned that climbers sometimes leave their rucksacks at the bottom of a climb for a few hours before returning to them. This gives the ravens plenty of time to undo clips and zips on the rucksacks to access any food that might be inside. They're also quite able to peck through the material of a rucksack to find food.

The ravens on Ben Nevis worked out how to find food in climbers' rucksacks in the winter of 2021. Who knows if they were taught by ravens from Glen Coe or if they worked it out for themselves, but they've learned quickly and are now experts at rucksack raiding. I've watched ravens attacking rucksacks half-buried in the snow and seen the contents scattered down the snow slopes. Be very wary of leaving your rucksack alone; it is being watched.

## Climbing protection

For protection on steep ground, a full rack of wires, hexes and ice screws is required. Camming devices are sometimes useful, but caution should be applied to their placement in icy and sometimes dubious rock. The current trend is to minimise the use of pegs, although you might consider carrying a few in case of emergency. Be aware, though, that too much gear will weigh you down and slow the day. Only take what's required for the route. On Tower Ridge a set of wires (sizes 1 to 10), two hexes, six extenders and four slings will usually be ample, while Point Five Gully will require six to eight ice screws, a set of wires and extenders. Belay anchors are usually on rock, but big ice routes (such as Orion Direct, Indicator Wall, etc) demand belaying on ice screws. More experienced climbers are obvious by their small but very well considered rack. Half ropes of 50 or 60m are recommended.

## ADDITIONAL SAFETY PRECAUTIONS

### Emergency shelters

There's only one emergency shelter on Ben Nevis and it's on the summit (grid ref NN 16684 71256). This should be kept for use only in an emergency. Please remember to close the door of the shelter when leaving – in a blizzard it fills with snow very quickly.

### Route cards

As an aid to potential rescue, climbers should leave a note of their intended route and return time with a reliable person in the valley. The police will be happy to take a note for you as long as you 'clock off' on your safe return. This is a very simple and wise precaution to take.

## USING THIS GUIDE

Each area of climbs has an overview description, as well as an info box which provides the following: approach start point, route lengths, approach time, crag base altitude, route styles, and details of avalanche risk. There are also approach and descent directions provided for each set of climbs.

The climbs are then described individually under headings which include name, route length, overall and technical grade, star rating and climbing style category. First-ascent details are provided where available. The route of each climb is shown on a photo topo unless otherwise indicated.

### Style categories

Every route in this guide is assigned a category to indicate the overall style of that route. There are three basic categories: snow, ice and mixed.

Of course, almost all winter routes will have snow on them. However, only when snow is significant to the overall character of the

## USING THIS GUIDE

## Climb style categories

- 🧗 snow ice
- 🧗 cascade ice
- 🧗 rocky mixed
- ◆ snow
- 🧗 snow patch cascade
- 🧗 turfy mixed
- 🧗 mixed
- 🧗 thin ice
- 🧗 icy mixed

route (mainly the easier gully lines) is the snow  category used.

Ice climbs are categorised as: snow-ice, cascade, snow patch cascade and thin face.

Mixed climbs are categorised as: general mixed, rocky mixed, turfy mixed and icy mixed.

General mixed climbs have a combination of rock, ice and turf with varying amounts of each of these ingredients. For climbs that particularly rely on one or more of these ingredients, this book uses the sub-categories of turfy mixed climb, icy mixed climb and rocky mixed climb to highlight that you want to have good conditions for these elements.

In some cases, two symbols are used. If a route has sections which

*Stob Bàn, Glen Nevis*

have very different styles, both of which add something significant to the feel of the route, then two symbols are used. For example, Gemini on Ben Nevis has significant cascade ice pitches followed by mixed pitches. This route is classified as cascade ice 🧊 **and** mixed 🔷.

There are various routes in this guide where the whole character of the route can change depending on conditions. There are some routes that are usually climbed as mixed routes, but which sometimes form ice and feel much more akin to an ice route. For example, Number Two Gully on Ben Nevis starts out the winter with a couple of pitches of ice but banks out with snow later on. So, it's classified as ice 🧊 **or** snow ❄. Thompson's Route on Ben Nevis is usually an icy mixed 🔶 climb but late in the season it can build so much ice that it's climbed entirely on ice and feels like an ice climb; this is classified as icy mixed 🔶 **or** ice 🧊.

The dynamic and ever-changing nature of the environment is one of the appealing aspects of Scottish winter climbing. The same route can feel very different under different conditions. For this reason, it would be impossible to accurately describe all the possible conditions that could be found on a particular route. Therefore, this classification, a bit like winter grades, is meant only as a rough guide to indicate what's likely to be found most of the time.

### Approach times

The times given in info boxes represent the time taken to walk from the most convenient parking place to the foot of the crag for average climbers on an average day. If it's very windy or there's deep snow cover, expect the walk in to take longer. Stops for rests, navigation or for gearing up will be in addition to the times given. Everyone walks at a different pace, of course, so don't see the time given as a challenge! Instead it will give you an idea of how much effort is required to reach the crags, which should help you choose the best place to climb.

### Grades

The current two-tier grading system developed by the Scottish Mountaineering Club (SMC) is used throughout this guide. As in previous systems, the higher the number, the more difficult the climb. The grades of I and II can be considered as introductory; only experienced climbers should attempt grades higher than this.

The grades are for 'average' conditions, and it should be remembered that winter climbs can vary enormously, depending on snow or ice build-up and the weather. Early in the season, when conditions can be lean, certain routes – particularly on ice – will be harder than later on when a good plating covers blank stretches and improves the conditions. Mixed routes, by comparison with snow and

## OVERALL GRADES

The following list provides an approximate definition of the overall grades. It's assumed that a rope is always used.

- **Grade I:** Climbs for which only one axe and crampons are normally required; either snow gullies around 45 degrees or easy ridges. Cornices can present problems and the avalanche hazard is always greatest in grade I gullies.
- **Grade II:** A second tool should be carried because of steep snow, difficult cornices and the occasional short ice pitch. Difficulties are usually short. Ridges at this grade will normally be straightforward scrambles in the summer.
- **Grade III:** More sustained and often steeper than grade II. Sometimes short and technical, particularly for mixed ascents of moderate rock climbs.
- **Grade IV:** Steep ice, from short vertical steps to long sections of 60–70 degrees. The mixed climbs require more advanced techniques such as axe 'torquing' and 'hooking'.
- **Grade V:** Sustained steep ice at 70–80 degrees with short vertical steps. Mixed climbing requires linked hard moves.
- **Grade VI:** Long vertical sections or thin and tenuous ice. Mixed routes include all that has gone before but more of it.
- **Grade VII:** Multi-pitch routes with long sections linking thin vertical ice and hard mixed moves, requiring strength, skill and stamina of the highest order.
- **Grade VIII:** By the time you tackle this grade and above you'll know exactly what's involved!

As a rough guideline to technical grades on ice, 3 = 60 degrees, 4 = 70 degrees, 5 = 80 degrees, 6 = vertical.

**Note:** A split grade such as II/III indicates the possibility of a wide variation in difficulties depending on condition, usually due to the possibility of great accumulations of snow over the course of the winter.

ice climbs, can benefit from lean, cold conditions, with no ice in the cracks.

The two-tier system shows a Roman numeral first, indicating the

# Winter Climbs: Glen Coe

overall seriousness of the climb, while the accompanying Arabic numeral represents the technical difficulty of the hardest sections of climbing. The aim of this system is to distinguish between routes with high levels of technical difficulty but which are less serious overall, and longer, more serious routes that might be less technically demanding.

- Point Five Gully (V,5) in average conditions is the benchmark from which other routes are graded.
- The overall grade takes into account all factors affecting the difficulty of reaching the top of the climb, including its technical difficulty, seriousness (frequency of protection and reliability of belays) and how sustained it is (length of hard sections of climbing and number of hard pitches).
- The technical grade reflects the difficulty of the hardest section(s) of climbing, without reference to seriousness. It is not intended to be used as a technical pitch-by-pitch grading. A technical grade of 5 indicates relatively straightforward, steep ice climbing; a technical grade of 6 generally indicates more technical mixed climbing or sustained vertical ice; technical grades of 7 and 8 indicate much more intricate and harder snowed-up rock moves.
- The technical grade normally varies by not more than two below or two above the overall grade. Thus V,5 can be taken as an average grade V route. A higher technical grade than the overall grade would indicate greater technical difficulty, offset by better protection (as frequently found on mixed routes); a lower technical grade would indicate greater seriousness.
- The overall difficulty is reflected in the overall grade, and just as in rock climbing where an E1 5a can be a more serious proposition than an E1 5c, a V,4 is not necessarily easier overall than a V,6.
- Climbs of up to grade III rarely have a technical grade; the overall grade is usually sufficient.

Some degree of variability undoubtedly occurs according to the prevailing conditions. While some climbs will nearly always be possible at close to the given grade, others require special (or even extraordinary) ice build-up, and the grades apply to such favourable situations. At other times these climbs may simply be non-existent. The grades of climbs in this guidebook have been decided after extensive consultation, but further comment is always valuable.

### Length of climb

Lengths of climbs and, where possible, pitch lengths are given in metres. Route lengths are as accurate as possible and will hopefully give the climber at least a reasonable idea of the scale of the route.

## Using this guide

### Recommended routes
Where possible, a three-star system has been used to indicate quality under good conditions – the more stars, the better the route. However, many unstarred routes under good conditions would warrant special mention. The star system will hopefully allow strangers to the area to find some good climbing on their first visit. Difficulty is not a prerequisite for stars; many simple climbs get a mention on the basis of their character, continuity, structure and adventure at the grade. All very subjective!

### Diagrams and route numbers
Nearly all cliffs have a corresponding diagram; for those without, the text is sufficient to locate a route. Lines marked on diagrams are as accurate as possible, but you should still use your judgement and the description to work out the best line to take in practice. Feedback is welcome. On some diagrams not all routes are shown, in order to avoid overcrowding. The routes shown offer good reference points for adjacent climbs that are not shown. On other diagrams, where there's space, routes are marked that are not described in the text. With an adventurous spirit, a line and a grade are all you need. An summary table of routes is included at the end of this guide.

### Appendices
Appendix A contains a list of useful contacts. Summary tables of climbs by area (in the same order in which they appear in the guide) – Appendix B – and by style – Appendix C – are provided for easy reference.

### AMENITIES

Fort William and Glencoe are well supplied with all the necessary facilities required by climbers.

#### Transport
Coaches travel daily to Fort William from Glasgow (passing through Glen Coe en route) and Inverness. Daily trains serve Fort William; it's common for climbers from London to catch the sleeper on a Friday evening, climb on Saturday and Sunday, then head back to work on the Sunday night train!

Glasgow and Inverness airports are both approximately two hours' drive from Fort William, with direct coach links.

From Fort William it's possible to start the approach to many areas by bike – especially if it's an e-bike. All types of bikes can be hired at Nevis Cycles (www.neviscycles.com) and Off Beat Bikes (www.offbeatbikes.co.uk). Cycling up to the top of the forest above North Face car park is hard work, but freewheeling back down at the end of the day makes it worthwhile.

The regular bus service to Glasgow that passes through Glen Coe can be used for climbs there.

However, most climbers find that a car is required to access the start points for each crag. For those arriving by public transport, cars can be hired in Fort William.

**Shops and food**

Specialist climbing gear can be bought in:
- Ellis Brigham, Fort William
- Nevisport, High Street, Fort William
- Cotswold Outdoor, High Street, Fort William
- The Ice Factor, Kinlochleven

Supermarkets in Claggan (NN 117 743) and Ballachulish (NN 083 583) stay open late. Fort William and the nearby village of Caol have chip shops. There are plenty of bars and restaurants. The Clachaig Inn in Glen Coe provides good bar meals and beer and is a favourite haunt of climbers. Several supermarkets in Fort William also stay open late most nights.

**Accommodation**

Good websites for finding local accommodation include:
- www.outdoorcapital.co.uk/stay
- http://fortwilliam-guesthouse.com

A number of climbing huts are available for bookings in the area from Crianlarich to Roybridge. One of these is owned and run by Mountaineering Scotland – the Alex MacIntyre Memorial Hut in Onich (www.mountaineering.scot/clubs/huts/national-huts). The CIC Hut on Ben Nevis is owned and run by the SMC and bookings can be made directly through them: www.smc.org.uk/huts/cic.

# GLEN COE

*Heading for the pinnacles on Aonach Eagach*

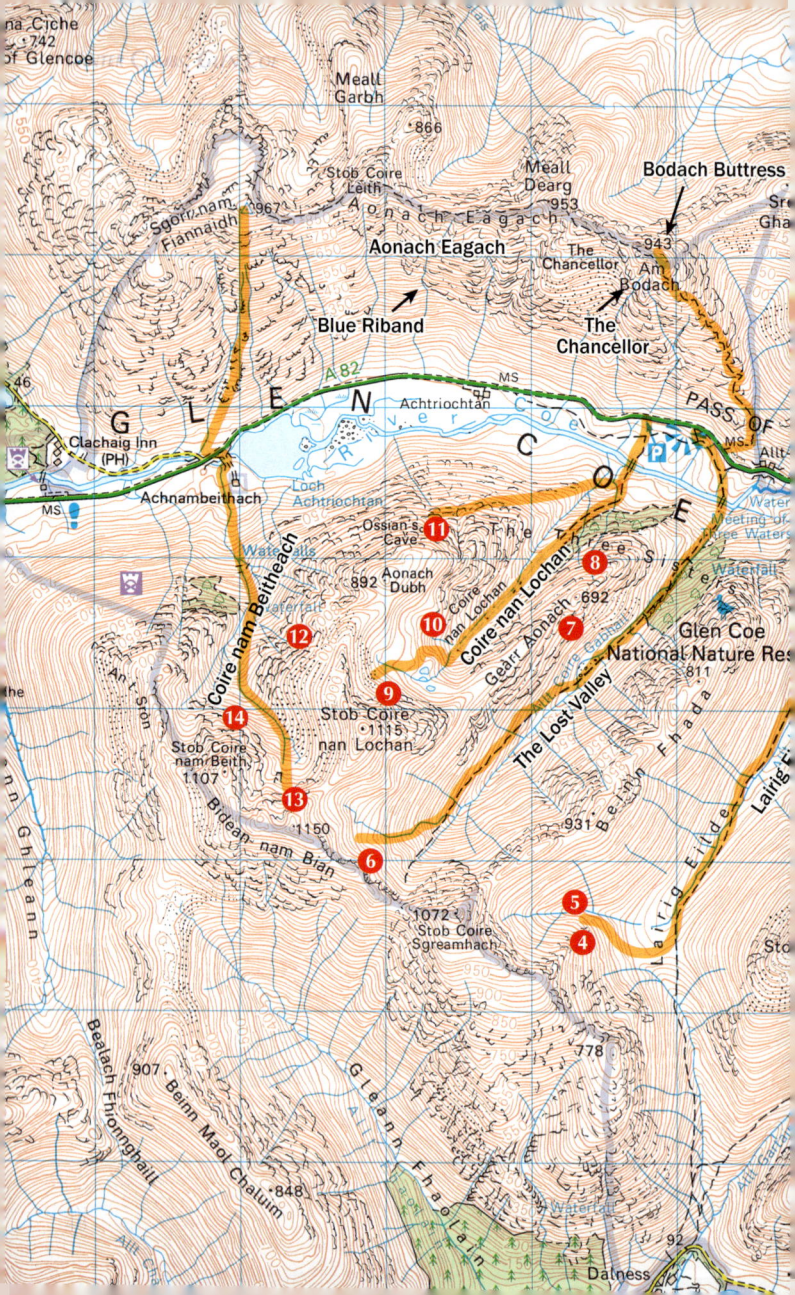

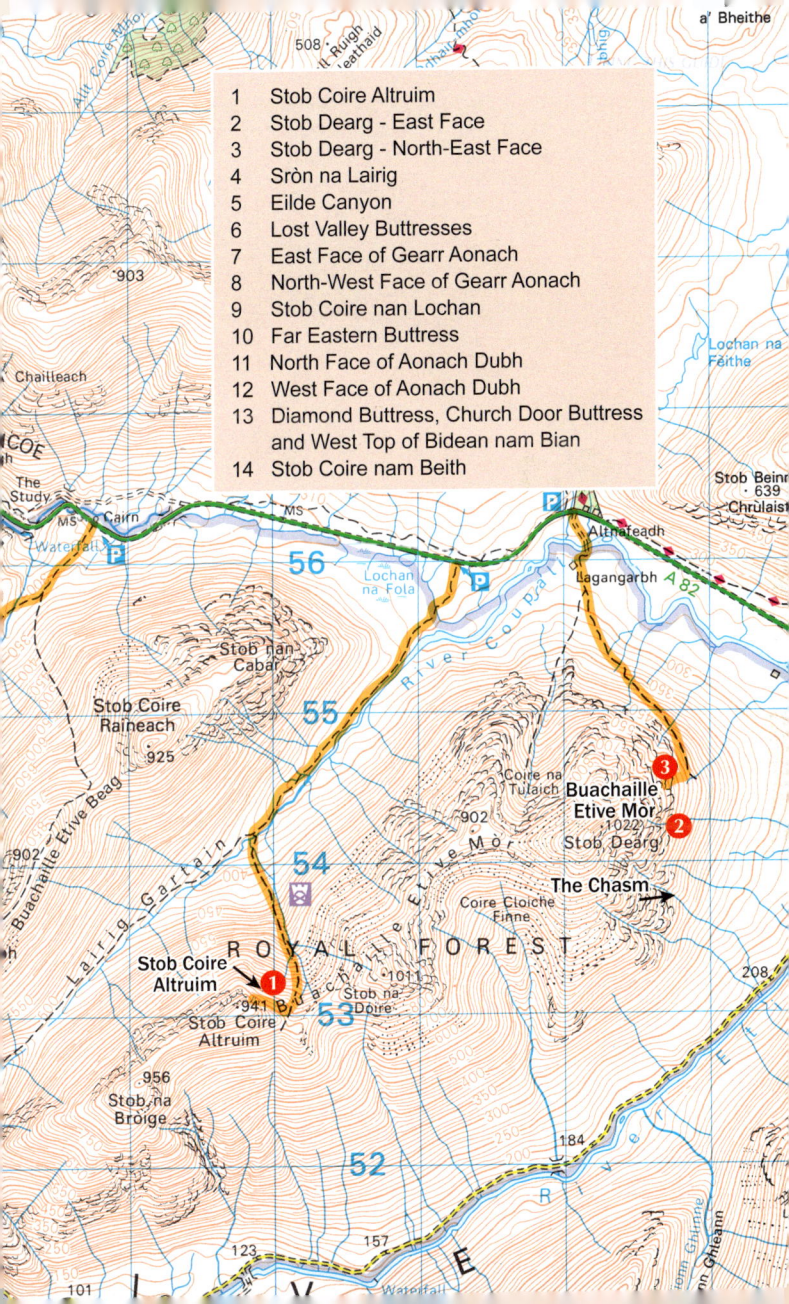

# Winter Climbs: Glen Coe

*Climbing Curved Ridge high above Rannoch Moor*

The varied and complex peaks of Glen Coe are all lower than those of Ben Nevis and the Aonachs, and good conditions are therefore less certain. Nonetheless, this area provides a wide range of route choice from mixed routes on the buttresses to cascade-style ice climbs. The ridges which abruptly separate the deep glens and corries are all fine outings, while the ridge and corrie walls provide excellent winter climbing to all standards. Only in recent years has Ben Nevis matched Glen Coe at the leading edge of modern mixed climbing on Scotland's west coast. The quality of the climbs here is very highly regarded.

Many climbs in Glen Coe are rocky mixed climbs requiring a good freeze and snow and rime to make the crags white. Generally, the ice climbing in Glen Coe is cascade ice climbing; frozen waterfalls and drainage lines which require a long period of sustained freeze at all levels. There are a few snow-ice gullies in Glen Coe which are very popular when in condition.

Another major advantage over Ben Nevis is the shorter approaches, especially when starting from higher up the glen. Some routes on Buachaille Etive Mòr, for example, can be started after only an hour's walk. Descent routes from all of the peaks should be treated with extreme care due to the steep and rocky nature of this area. The complex nature of the crags also allows the formation of small pockets of wind slab in many locations which can easily catch out unwary climbers. The area is well covered by either of two maps: OS Landranger Sheet 41 (1:50,000), or Harvey Superwalker, *Glen Coe* (1:25,000).

## Aonach Eagach 967m (Sgorr nam Fiannaidh)

| | |
|---|---|
| **Start** | Traversing from east to west, start at the lay-by on the north side of the A82 at NN 173 567 |
| **Time** | 1hr 45min to reach Am Bodach |
| **Crag base altitude** | 850m on Aonach Eagach; 350m for the cascade ice |
| **Route lengths** | 3km for the full traverse; 120–600m for climbs on the south flanks |
| **Route styles** | Classic rocky mixed ridge traverse, cascade ice and turfy mixed |
| **Avalanches** | Normally very unlikely on the ridge and south-facing descent |

Aonach Eagach is the long, notched ridge which bounds Glen Coe to the north, applying particularly to the narrow crest extending between Sgorr nam Fiannaidh on the west to Am Bodach at the east end. The Glen Coe flank of this ridge is steep and complex, very rocky and seamed by many gullies.

### Approach
A well-made path leads out of the start-point lay-by and winds up to Am Bodach along its south-east ridge. There's a rocky section with some scrambling about halfway up. Alternatively, cross the stream into the corrie to the east of Am Bodach and follow easy slopes to the top (943m).

### Descent
From Sgorr nam Fiannaidh, go due south down steep snow or scree slopes which lead to a narrow path running down to the Clachaig road junction with the main road. This descent is unrelentingly steep and bad for the knees but might save on the walk back to the starting point. Alternatively, descend from Sgorr nam Fiannaidh west then north-west to the saddle below the Pap of Glen Coe. From here, head west then south-west to NN 110 586, where the plantation meets the public road. It's very useful, if possible, to leave a vehicle in this vicinity (without blocking gates) and another at the eastern end of the ridge. The descent alongside Clachaig Gully, directly towards the hotel, should be avoided as it's extremely loose.

## Aonach Eagach Traverse 3km end to end III***

(no photo topo)

In good weather the ridge gives a very fine winter expedition. Speed is essential, so practise your Alpine skills of moving together on a rope along narrow ridges. It's often good to do this route after a big storm has put lots of soft snow on the ridge. A thin cover of wet snow or verglas on the rocks will make a traverse slow and tortuous.

The normal route is from east to west, which gives the advantage of 100m less to climb. The best starting point is from near the white cottage at Allt-na-reigh; parking is available just down the road (NN 173 567).

The descent from Am Bodach to the west can be quite difficult and intimidating, going down in three steps: on the middle step, go slightly right then back left and down a big groove with a pedestal block, by abseil if required. The ridge is much easier from the bottom of these three steps to Meall Dearg. The most interesting section is between Meall Dearg (953m) and Stob Coire Leith (940m) – particularly a very narrow pinnacled section and an awkward slabby descent beyond it.

It should borne in mind that there is no safe descent from the ridge on the Glen Coe (south) flank between the two end peaks of Am Bodach and Sgorr nam Fiannaidh. Very many accidents – some fatal – have occurred on these difficult

*Traversing the pinnacles*

and craggy slopes. There are one or two reasonable escape options to the north, leading to Loch Leven.

> Some fine cascade ice climbs form on the south flank of Aonach Eagach, below the pinnacles, during sustained freezing conditions. A small parking area at NN 153 572, or the bigger one 500 metres to the west, should be used. Climb the hillside due north to the foot of the route. Blue Riband is the obvious steep cascade with a pillar of ice at its base.

### Blue Riband 600m V,5***
*J. MacKenzie and G. Rooney, 18 February 1979*
Three ice falls lead to easier (grade 3) ice. Above this, there's one short and steep icefall to climb or avoid on the left before easy snow slopes lead to the top, which is just east of Aonach Eagach's pinnacles.

> Further up Glen Coe, the south side of Am Bodach is made up of dramatic buttresses and gullies high above the glen and running all the way up the mountainside. They face south, so they don't collect much snow and any sunshine melts it away quite quickly.

### Vice Chancellor Ridge 210m III**
*H. MacInnes and Glencoe School of Winter Climbing (GSWC), 18 February 1969*
The big buttress left of The Chancellor, starting at the foot of Big Chock Gully (III) which runs up the left side of The Chancellor. The buttress is climbed to an imposing tower, climbed by a central line. A third tower leads to narrow snow crests and slopes to the top.

### The Chancellor 400m IV**
*W. Skidmore and R.T. Richardson, December 1965*
The prominent buttress jutting out into Glen Coe south-west from the summit of Am Bodach. After a very good freeze and plenty of snow this makes a fine climb with a few tricky sections and one distinct crux up the front of the obvious tower. From the parking at NN 168 569, walk north-west then go north up the stream coming out of Old Man Gully. Follow the west bank of this to the foot of the buttress. Find your way up the turfy, mossy buttress with an excursion to the left and back to the crest before the steep tower. Easy but narrow, beautiful crests lead to the top.

### Chancellor Gully 500m III/IV**

*H. MacInnes, 1960*
(no photo topo)
The big obvious gully running up and then leftwards, up the south face of Am Bodach. It is directly above the parking at NN 168 569 and turns left below the vertical chimney called The Slit. Walk up the east bank of the stream and get into the gully below The Slit. You might need to go up the left bank of the gully at first to find the water-ice that will lead to the top in lots of pitches.

### Bodach Buttress 120m III,4*

*A. Nelson and A. Hogarth, 30 December 2017*
(no photo topo)
This is the north buttress dropping straight down from the summit of Am Bodach. Walk up Coire an Ruigh to reach the col at 816m, north-east of the summit. Traverse across the slope to find the buttress and climb it in four pitches over slabby rock and useful patches of turf.

# BUACHAILLE ETIVE MÒR

## *Stob Dearg 1022m (NN 223 543)*

| | |
|---|---|
| **Start** | Altnafeadh on the A82 (NN 220 563) |
| **Time** | 1hr 30min |
| **Crag base altitude** | 600m |
| **Route lengths** | 60–1000m |
| **Route styles** | Mixed climbing and some snow-ice |
| **Avalanches** | Crowberry Basin and Great Gully are both notorious for avalanches. |

Buachaille Etive Mòr is a long ridge with four tops. Stob Dearg is the north top – a beautifully symmetrical cone standing dominantly over Rannoch Moor. This might be the most photographed mountain in Scotland, and rightly so. It's the highest of the four tops, the only one that gives much climbing, and it's generally referred to as 'The Buachaille'.

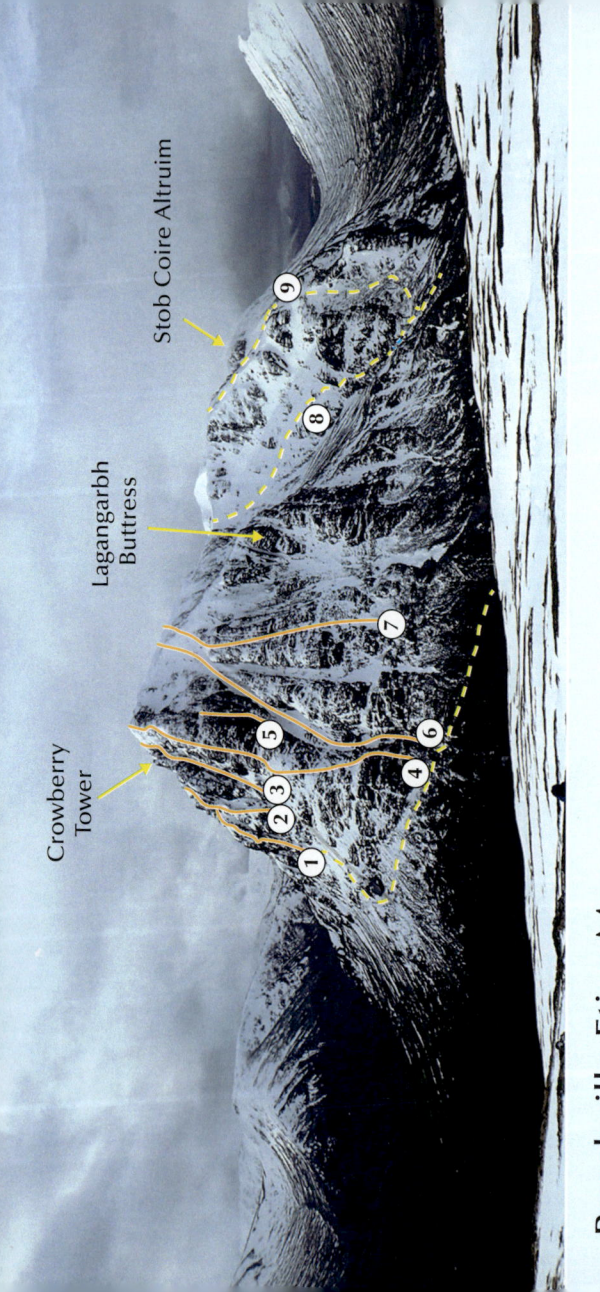

# Buachaille Etive Mor

1. D Gully Buttress IV,4**
2. Curved Ridge III,3***
3. Crowberry Gully IV,4***
4. North Buttress IV,4***
5. Raven's Gully V,6***
6. Great Gully II/III
7. Ephemeron Gully IV/4*
8. Coire na Tulaich descent
9. West Ridge descent

The mountain is an excellent summer rock-climbing area, while in winter its natural ridge and gully lines are among the best in Scotland. The view from the area surrounding Curved Ridge is one of the most striking panoramas from any British hill.

The most popular routes are all on the central section of the mountain above the Waterslide Slab, but many fine climbs can be found on the area overlooking Glen Etive between D Gully Buttress and The Chasm.

For climbers new to this area it's advisable to drive along the main road towards the Kingshouse in order to view the main features of the mountain before choosing a route; or to drive down Glen Etive for a mile or so in order to decipher the various routes on the complicated face of Central Buttress.

### Approach
The River Coupall is crossed by a bridge leading to Lagangarbh. Some 150 metres beyond the hut, a path leads south-eastwards, gradually rising, to cross the foot of Great Gully after about 1.5km. Immediately after Great Gully, a path goes straight up to climb the lower easy part of North Buttress with some scrambling. This approach to North Buttress can also be used to reach Shelf Route and Naismith's Route by bearing left towards Crowberry Ridge.

The usual way to Crowberry Basin follows the path from Great Gully around the foot of North Buttress, rising slowly to meet the Waterslide. From this slab, ascend straight up the steep and loose scree slopes to its left. From the top of the screes, a traverse up and right must be made above steep rocky ground in order to gain the foot of Crowberry Gully or Curved Ridge. Routes to the left (south) of D Gully Buttress can be reached by traversing left from near the top of the screes, or approached from the Glen Etive road.

### Descent
There's only one reasonable descent route in winter. From the summit (NN 22363 54311), follow the fairly level ridge for 300 metres bearing 250° grid, or to NN 22104 54113. Then change course to 270° grid and descend to reach a shallow cairned col (NN 21637 54157) at the head of **Coire na Tulaich**. This section can be particularly difficult in white-out conditions. There are occasional cairns, but it may be necessary to stay roped up and take both front and back bearings to keep on course. The most common mistake is to continue too far south-west and descend into Glen Etive; this slope is not too difficult, but it's a long walk back on the road. Care should

be taken not to stray to the north too early, as there are some large crags at the head of Coire na Tulaich.

From the col, a steep initial slope leads down into the corrie. This slope is often avalanche prone and might have a cornice above it. A number of significant, fatal avalanches have taken place in this area.

There's a path down the left-hand side of the lower corrie above the gorge (west side), which leads easily down to Lagangarbh and the road. If the gorge is full of hard snow it makes an easy descent, but is also a big terrain trap for avalanches coming down from any direction.When the avalanche risk in Coire na Tulaich is too high, it's possible to avoid the corrie by ascending slightly from the col to point 902m (NN 214 542) and descending north by the ridge to the west of Coire na Tulaich. All the large outcrops on this **west ridge** descent are avoidable by moving left.

The routes are described from left to right.

## STOB DEARG FROM GLEN ETIVE – EAST FACE

The area between Central Buttress and The Chasm is both complicated and huge in scale, requiring good judgement and climbing skills. There are no particularly easy exits until the summit of Curved Ridge is reached. This section of the mountain is recommended for experienced climbers who savour the challenge of long routes with an 'Alpine' feel. Due to its south-easterly aspect, this part of the mountain receives any sunshine on offer which can create good snow-ice, or give you soggy snow or strip the snow altogether. Snow conditions can change as height is gained, and a wary eye should be kept on the potential for avalanches.

### The Chasm 450m V,6***

(no photo topo)

This route is approached from the Glen Etive road (NN 233 531), 2.5km from the main road junction. At this point two streams can be seen joining by the road on the map; The Chasm drains into the northmost of these. The route forms an obvious gulch on the hillside to the right (west), and is blessed with a short approach.

During winters of heavy snowfall to very low levels, this climb may be a bit easier. In leaner conditions several pitches will be faced to get up, over or around various chockstones, and the nature of the climb becomes hard and

## Stob Dearg East Face

1. The Chasm to Crowberry Traverse II*
2. North Face Route V,6**
3. Alpen V,5*
4. D Gully Buttress IV,4**
5. Curved Ridge III,3***
6. Agag's Groove VII,7***
7. North Buttress IV,4***

Lady's Gully IV,4**

time-consuming. Several variations exist higher up the gully, with the direct continuation being the most difficult and rarely completed. Escapes from the gully can be made at a number of points, most easily to the left.

### The Chasm to Crowberry Traverse 1000m II*

Easily seen from the Glen Etive road, this expedition starts at the right edge of The Chasm at an altitude of around 550m. An obvious feature is an undercut cave at the halfway mark. The line can be followed towards the top of Curved Ridge, or harder and more direct variants taken towards the summit. An excellent day out for explorers!

> Left of D Gully Buttress is Central Buttress, and the two are separated by a wide-open bay, from the back of which springs a line of chimneys and small gullies. An approach towards Central Buttress can be made by continuing horizontally on a faint track for a further 500 metres from the Waterslide Slab mentioned in the approach to the Crowberry Basin. This approach will put the climber below the rocks of Central Buttress.

### Lady's Gully 240m IV,4**

*J.R. Marshall, I.D. Haig and G.J. Ritchie (Left Fork), 24 February 1957*

Easily seen on the hillside to the west of the stream junction (NN 240 537), this gully is the first one north of The Chasm. It can be approached by continuing left from the Waterslide Slab on the Curved Ridge approach path. It is not often in good condition, but when it is (during winters of heavy snowfall and a long, sustained freeze), the climbing is very good. Follow the line of the gully to a steep wall (45m). Climb the wall, which can be difficult (45m), and several more difficult pitches to a fork in the gully. The left fork is the best option. This leads to easier ground beneath the summit ridge. Finish either by gaining the summit or by traversing left above The Chasm and descending into Glen Etive. If the right fork is followed, the top of Curved Ridge can be gained beneath Crowberry Tower.

### Direct Route 95m IV*

*T. McAulay and D. Sanderson, 21 January 1984*
(no photo topo)

This route lies on the south face of Central Buttress and is reached by traversing left under the buttress's lowest rocks beneath a distinctive yellow cave and climbing up to a small pinnacle. Pass the pinnacle on the right or left and climb to a ledge, which is followed up right to a 6m chimney, and follow this to Heather Ledge. Descend from Heather Ledge as described in the following route.

### Kinloss Corner 120m V,6**

*A. Paul and D. Sanderson, January 1984*
(no photo topo)
A short, technical and sustained route which starts 15m left of and below North Face Route, where a slab leads to a corner. Climb the slab and corner, and a second easier slab leading to a short open corner. Climb this corner then a rib on the left of another corner, which leads to an easier ledge (Heather Ledge). It's possible to traverse right on the ledge and either abseil or climb down rightwards to easier ground between Central Buttress and D Gully Buttress.

### North Face Route 220m V,6**

*J.R. Marshall and J. Stenhouse, January 1958*
A sustained and difficult mixed route. Climb a series of steep corners, walls, chimneys and cracks on the right side (north-east edge) of Central Buttress. These lead to an easier-angled ledge (Heather Ledge). A large white scar may be seen on the north face above, with a recess beneath it. Gain the recess by traversing round two pillars. Continue the traverse rightwards, descending to a ledge. Climb an awkward 3m wall to a right-slanting ledge, which is followed to a 20m chimney. Climb the chimney to gain a platform, then traverse left to a short steep crack near the north-east edge. Follow the edge to the top. Traverse rightwards across the top of D Gully onto Curved Ridge.

### Alpen 245m V,5*

*S. Belk, I. Fulton, K.V. Crocket and C. Stead, March 1972*
This route follows the chimneys and small gullies as mentioned above to the left of D Gully Buttress. Start halfway up an easy gully which trends left between D Gully Buttress and Central Buttress, at the foot of a wall. Climb steep turf ledges to the foot of a corner (45m). Continue up the corner to a cave belay (20m). Climb the right wall of the cave (10m), then a chimney, and trend more easily left to a small spike belay (40m). Traverse left and belay below the right-hand of two parallel chimneys (15m). Climb this chimney and rightward ramp to a belay (40m). Move up left in the gully (40m) and finish up right to the buttress top (45m).

# Stob Dearg North East Face

① North Face Route V,6**
② D Gully Buttress IV,4**
③ Curved Ridge III,3***
④ Agag's Groove VII,7***
⑤ Crowberry Gully IV,4***
⑥ North Buttress IV,4***

---

**STOB DEARG – NORTH-EAST FACE**

### D Gully Buttress 150m IV,4**

The buttress is narrow, and defined on the right by the deep D Gully and on the left by indefinite rocks merging with Central Buttress, with which it forms a right angle. Start to the left of the foot of D Gully. A prominent steep smooth step high up the buttress is a useful landmark.

The first section is fairly easy apart from one steep short wall climbed by good cracks. The way is then blocked by the steep smooth step. Go left of this and climb a chimney and gully leading back rightwards to regain the crest, very narrow at this point. Above, a long slabby section gives the crux, climbed on the left or (harder and not well protected) at its right edge overlooking D Gully. After a further 30m or so the buttress ends on a shoulder. Traverse right to gain Curved Ridge below its crux tower.

## Curved Ridge 300m III,3***
*G.T. Glover and R.G. Napier, 11 April 1898*

A magnificent route and by far the most popular to the summit of the mountain. It passes through grand rock scenery, is a good general viewpoint and gives interesting climbing under almost any conditions (it is especially well sheltered from a south-westerly gale). It is certainly the most useful winter climb on Buachaille and can be quite hard.

From the top of the screes on the approach, traverse up and right, heading for a small stream. Cross the stream and move up into Crowberry Basin. Climb the left side of Crowberry Basin to find the foot of Curved Ridge.

The line follows the crest of the ridge throughout, beneath Rannoch Wall, the very steep side of Crowberry Ridge. Two short steep pitches at the start lead to a long easier section. Another two pitches up a tower with a distinctive corner on the second pitch lead to a cairn at the top of Curved Ridge and below the foot of Crowberry Tower. From the cairn a horizontal left traverse for about 30 metres brings you onto a snow slope with two gully exits:

1   The gully slanting back to the right reaches Crowberry Tower Gap and from there a short groove leads left then right to the top of Crowberry Gully and the final summit slopes.
2   The gully going up slightly leftward leads directly to the summit rocks. It is probably the quickest but not the most interesting way and it has the greatest avalanche potential.

If time permits, an ascent of the Crowberry Tower can be included if the first route is followed. From the gap, a short corner is climbed to a ledge on the left, then an easy rising spiral traverse leads to the top. There are more interesting routes up the tower, but this is the easiest and best in descent.

**Beware:** there's currently a 4m-high block perched on the side of Crowberry Tower overlooking Crowberry Gully. The base of the block is already undercut and is falling away slowly. Eventually, this block will fall off down Crowberry Gully, wiping out everything in its way.

## Route I 70m V,6*
*H. MacInnes and partner, February 1972*
(no photo topo)

The natural line of weakness in the middle of Rannoch Wall (the dominant rock wall to the right of Curved Ridge), starting 15m above the cave pitch in Easy Gully to the right of Curved Ridge. Climb a chimney and trend right up a slanting narrow shelf to slabs under a 4m wall. Climb the wall (crux) and the long upper groove back left.

Shelf Route

1. Naismith's Route 200m IV,5*
2. Shelf Route 200m IV,6**

Crowberry Gully

### Agag's Groove 105m VII,7***
*H. MacInnes, C. Bonington, K. MacPhail and G. McIntosh, 8 February 1953*
The obvious corner ramp line cutting up and left across Rannoch Wall on the left side of Crowberry Tower. This is a very good and highly regarded rock climb in summer and should be kept undamaged by winter ascents. Only attempt an ascent in perfect winter conditions (frozen solid and covered in rime and snow). Start at a detached block at the bottom right side of Rannoch Wall. Climb the deepening corner in two pitches to a block belay and good ledge (60m). Climb the ramp above and step left to climb the nose up a steep hidden crack (25m), or climb the ramp and continuation groove direct (harder). Traverse left and follow corners to the top.

### Naismith's Route 200m IV,5*
From the narrows at the foot of Crowberry Gully proper, move left onto the obvious Pinnacle Ledge at the foot of two chimneys. The left-hand chimney is followed. Climb up to the right and as soon as possible take the easiest line back left to the crest. Continue up the crest with easing difficulty to Crowberry Tower.

### Shelf Route 200m IV,6**
*W.M. MacKenzie and W.H. Murray, March 1937*
A superb and sustained climb if good conditions are present; this is a shallow chimney line running up the left wall of Crowberry Gully. Start low down in Crowberry Gully and traverse left to the foot of two chimneys. Climb the right wall and rib of the left chimney to a shallow trough above. Follow the scoop above between the steep left wall and a small pinnacle. The direct line continues to a recess under the pinnacle, from where an awkward right traverse is made to gain grooves which lead up to the ridge below Crowberry Tower. Either climb the tower direct and descend its right side to the col (Crowberry Gap) or traverse left towards the top of Curved Ridge.

### Crowberry Gully 300m IV,4***
*H. Raeburn, W.A. Brigg and H.S. Tucker, April 1909*
A magnificent classic climb of considerable quality, Crowberry Gully can also be dangerous due to avalanches. Conditions vary remarkably and can change in a short space of time. It may be completely banked up with snow except for an ice pitch at the Junction (where a rightwards rising traverse is made from the foot of the deep recessed Left Fork) and another pitch at the exit from a cave near the top of the gully. The Cave will usually give the crux of the normal route, climbed by the right wall on ice and 10–15m in height. If attempted when out of condition (particularly early in the season) there could be many more pitches,

and Junction and Cave pitches may be all but impossible with only a thin veneer of verglas.

The Left Fork (**IV,5**\*\**C.M.G. Smith, R.J. Taunton and I.C. Robertson, 18 March 1949*) leads steeply out of the main gully to Crowberry Tower Gap. The deeply recessed gully soon becomes a narrow iced chimney, which is capped by a large overhanging block. The capstone will always be difficult, but good protection is available. On the first ascent, the third member of the party could not be pulled over the capstone after the second man had stood on his head to gain elevation!

**Beware:** there's currently a 4m-high block perched on the side of Crowberry Tower overlooking Crowberry Gully. The base of the block is already undercut and is falling away slowly. Eventually, this block will fall off down Crowberry Gully, wiping out everything in its way.

### North East Zig-Zag 100m III*
*J.R. Marshall, A.H. Hendry and G.J. Ritchie, 1957*
(no photo topo)
An interesting climb in open surroundings which has many variations and is clear of the avalanche problems associated with Crowberry Gully. Start from the left end of a broad terrace above and right of Crowberry Gully. Move up left and then back right by the simplest line to gain the upper section of North Buttress.

### North Buttress 300m IV,4*** or
This takes the line of chimneys splitting the middle section of the huge buttress to the left of Great Gully and right of Crowberry Gully. Just after crossing Great Gully on the path, turn right and scramble up slabby ground with steeper sections to two prominent boulders. Carry on up to the foot of the chimneys. After 160m these lead onto easier-angled slopes with the odd difficult step.

The climb itself is possible in virtually any conditions and is safe from avalanche once on the route. It is most commonly found as a rocky mixed climb but it holds a lot of snow which can turn to nice snow-ice.

### Raven's Gully 135m V,6***
*H. MacInnes and C. Bonington, 14 February 1953*
The dark slit high up on the North Buttress (left) wall of Great Gully. This is a classic climb but not often sufficiently banked out with snow these days. When in condition the crux is soon reached – a large chockstone. The lower chockstones need to be well banked out with hard snow to make this climb feasible. Above, three or four long difficult pitches lead to the top, finding a way up to the left of the upper chimney. The Direct Finish climbs straight up the upper chimney with some exciting bridging.

*Climbing Raven's Gully on Buachaille Etive Mòr*

A descent of Great Gully Buttress or the gully between this and Broad Buttress can be made after finishing Raven's Gully. This is only advised if avalanche potential is low.

### Raven's Edge 170m VII,7***
*R. Anderson and R. Milne, 30 March 1996*
(no photo topo)
Start at the foot of Raven's Gully and go right, up a line just right of the edge overlooking Raven's Gully, then left around a projecting rib to a belay at the top of a shallow left-facing corner (55m). Climb up left, then down to a thin traverse leading to the foot of the corner, 6m above the gully (15m). Go up to the roof, step down to traverse the wall, then up left to the foot of the 'open book' corner which is climbed to a belay at its top (35m). Ascend a corner above and traverse left beneath the roof (possible thread-belay). Continue around the edge to a better-placed thread-belay (35m). Climb the deep crack up left (30m) followed by a short wall.

### Cuneiform Buttress, Ordinary Route 135m IV,5
*J.R. Marshall, D.N. Mill and G.J. Ritchie, 15 December 1957*
(no photo topo)
Start at the lowest rocks near the foot of Raven's Gully and climb to a broad terrace. From its right end, climb a short steep pitch followed by grooves to another

broad ledge beneath the vertical upper section of the cliff. Traverse right around an exposed edge onto the west face. Climb an obvious shelf then turn towards the centre of the cliff, which is climbed to the top. A right-hand start (*M. Hind and R. Webb, 2 January 2003*) climbs the obvious right-hand fault to the terrace, 60m IV,4.

### The Long Chimney 135m IV**
*R. Smith and D. Leaver, 15 December 1957*
(no photo topo)
Follow the Ordinary Route (described above) to the broad terrace, then traverse hard right and climb the long obvious shallow chimney.

### Great Gully 360m II/III
*N. Collie, 1894*
The first deep gully to cross the path about 20min from Lagangarbh. It is sometimes confused with easier gullies further west. Early in the season it can give several good pitches of cascade ice, but it sometimes banks out and often has considerable avalanche danger.

> To the right (west) of Great Gully is Great Gully Buttress (II/III). The next buttress to the right is Broad Buttress (III).

### Ephemeron Gully 340m IV,4*
*K.V. Crocket, A. Walker and P. Craig, 28 December 1985*
This route is immediately on the right (west) side of Broad Buttress and follows a line of icy grooves. Descent can be made over the top of Lagangarbh Buttress.

> **LAGANGARBH BUTTRESS NN 222 548**
>
> The most westerly buttress on the north face of Buachaille Etive Mòr. Its west face overlooks Coire na Tulaich.

### Lagangarbh Chimney 60m III,4**
On the west face of Lagangarbh Buttress, this climb starts about halfway up the gully to the right of the buttress.

## COIRE NA TULAICH

This is the corrie used by most people in descent from routes on Buachaille Etive Mòr and is the normal route of ascent to the top for walkers. In this corrie there are good opportunities for cascade ice climbing and mixed climbing when a short approach is required or the conditions on the higher crags are affected by bad weather. Do, however, be careful if the avalanche hazard is considerable or high, as a number of significant, fatal slides have taken place in this area.

## *Stob Coire Altruim 941m (NN 197 530)*

| | |
|---|---|
| **Start** | Large lay-by on the A82 at NN 212 559 |
| **Time** | 2hr |
| **Crag base altitude** | 850m |
| **Route lengths** | 100m |
| **Route styles** | Turfy mixed climbing |
| **Avalanches** | The long slope underneath the crag can avalanche and runout all the way to cross the approach path. |

This is the third top of Buachaille Etive Mòr when approaching from Stob Dearg and it has a north-east-facing crag very close to the summit. It's reached by a steep pull up from Lairig Gartain. The big steep slope beneath the crag can avalanche down to the bottom at 500m.

**Approach**
Follow the path south-west up Lairig Gartain. Cross the stream after 2.5km, then follow a path south and up into Coire Altruim. Climb high into the corrie before traversing right to the foot of the crags.

**Descent**
Walk south-east to the col at the top of Coire Altruim and descend the corrie.

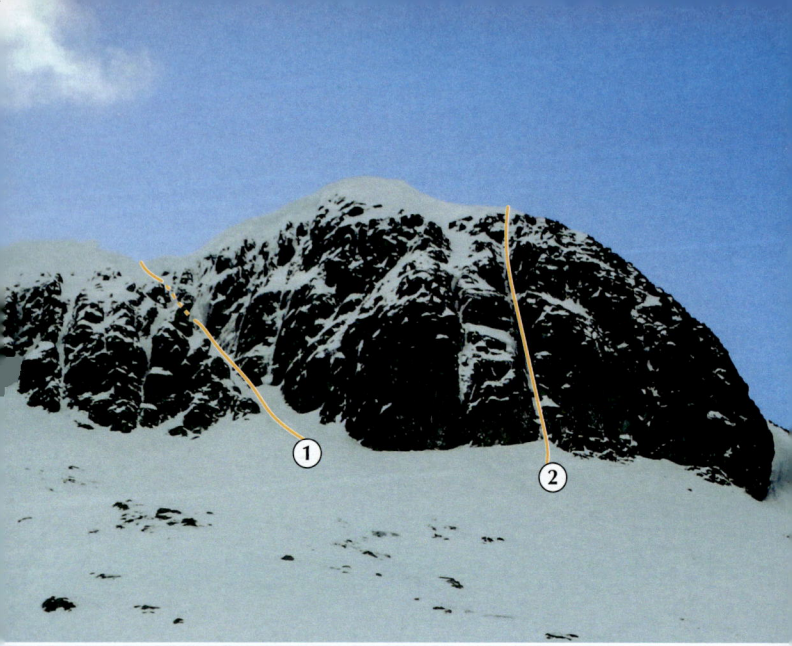

# Stob Coire Altruim

① Central Couloir III
② Dalmation Couloir IV***

**Central Couloir 100m III**
*J.G. Brown and J.G. Parish, 23 February 1950*
The biggest gully in the crag, to the left of the main buttress. Fork left towards the top.

**Dalmation Couloir 100m IV*****
*G.E. Little and A. Baker, 2 March 1991*
Climb the obvious deep chimney in the centre of the buttress with a similar feel to Raven's Gully. A very good freeze is required to make the first pitch viable.

# LAIRIG EILDE

*Sròn na Lairig and Eilde Canyon*

| | |
|---|---|
| **Start** | Just east of The Study at the car park opposite the big cairn (NN 187 562) |
| **Time** | 1hr 45min |
| **Crag base altitude** | 600m |
| **Route lengths** | 30–300m |
| **Route styles** | Turfy mixed climbing and cascade ice |
| **Avalanches** | Generally OK but be aware of the big slopes leading down towards the canyon on both sides and the natural terrain trap of the canyon itself. |

The glen between Buachaille Etive Beag and Beinn Fhada is the home of a classic mountaineering ridge and cascade ice climbs.

### Approach
Follow the path south-west and fork right after 600 metres to cross Allt Lairig Eilde. This stream is often too high to cross in winter, in which case follow its south-east bank. Follow the path all the way to the lairig (pass) at NN 170 534 and walk west then north-west to the foot of the ridge.

### Descent
From the top of Sròn na Lairig, continue up to Stob Coire Sgreamhach and descend its north-east ridge, with a steep step 200m down from the summit, then traverse Beinn Fhada and go down its east flank. Alternatively, walk down to the south-east towards point 778m, turning north-east to return to the lairig.

### Sròn na Lairig (NN 163 535) 300m II**
*Baird and Coulson, and Allbery, Kendall and Wedderburn, March 1934*
A prominent rocky spur overlooking the head of Lairig Eilde and leading up onto the south-east ridge of Stob Coire Sgreamhach gives a fine climb. The approach up the Lairig is quite long but gentle. The lower part is best avoided on the left, but higher up it narrows to a fine crest.

# Lairig Eilde

Eilde Canyon

① Sròn na Lairig II**

*Sròn na Lairig, high above Lairig Eilde*

### Eilde Canyon (NN 164 536)

Discovered as a cascade ice climbing venue in 2010, the main canyon is around 250 metres long and 10–15 metres wide. Most of the routes are formed by streams dropping into the canyon, and are 30–40 metres long. It's very sheltered from the wind but might be avalanche prone. It requires a good freeze and is likely to form in the same way as the climbs at Beinn Udlaidh.

About 20 separate climbs have been recorded, mostly at grade IV or V, with just a few easier climbs. Take a big bunch of ice screws and a couple of warthogs, 60m ropes (belay anchors can be set far back), and sharp picks!

#### NORTH-EAST FACE OF BEINN FHADA

The following routes lie on the north-east face of Beinn Fhada. Easily seen from the road and with a short approach, these cascade ice climbs offer good sport when freezing levels are low. Walk in from The Study or Lairig Eilde, parking at NN 188 562. Descent from most routes can be made by abseil; or continue up until you can descend the east flank.

### The Bubble 60m III/IV,4***

*S. Kennedy, C. Macleod and M. Slater, 2 January 1982*
(no photo topo)
Well seen from the road if in condition, at approximately NN 177 556. A good little route. The icefall to its right has also been climbed at grade III.

A selection of six independent cascade ice climbs can be found above the big gully starting at NN 175 560, all at about grade IV,4 and 150m long. This area is well worth a visit and is unlikely to be crowded. A long hard freeze is required. The easiest approach is to follow the east side of the stream downhill from Hamish MacInnes' old cottage at Allt-na-ruigh (NN 175 566), then go uphill to the big gully. Cars should be left in the lay-bys 500 metres west.

# THE LOST VALLEY (COIRE GABHAIL)

The left-hand corrie between the Three Sisters is a spectacular and historic place. It's worth a visit just to see its incredible geography, and it also offers a wide variety of good climbs that can be quite well sheltered from the wind.

The path into the corrie leads through a gorge, eventually crossing the stream then a built path, to reach corrie floor – a flat 500 metres of shingle and grass (45min). The gorge path is exposed to the drop to the stream and can be icy, in which case the path at a higher level is recommended and reached from the entrance to the gorge. At the entrance to the corrie floor is a 10m boulder – a useful landmark.

Beyond the corrie floor there are two paths to the right of the stream and at different levels. The highest is the better of the two and makes a gradual ascent along the side of the valley, with the cliffs of the east face of Gearr Aonach up to the right. Further up the path lie the Lost Valley Buttresses.

The cliffs of Stob Coire nan Lochan may also be reached by bearing back in a northerly direction, beyond the cliffs of the east face of Gearr Aonach, obliquely across the hillside to reach the shoulder where the ridge from Gearr Aonach rises steeply towards Stob Coire nan Lochan's summit.

### Beinn Fhada and Stob Coire Sgreamhach
A fine ridge crest runs between the peaks of Beinn Fhada and Stob Coire Sgreamhach, steep and rocky on all sides. Point 811m (NN 171 551) can be reached from 200 metres beyond the 10m boulder at the entrance to the Lost Valley (or from the east side). Take the line of least resistance and arrive at a bealach after 1hr 30min of upward toil.

The ridge is followed with continual interest to a rocky step (NN 157 538), which should be turned on the left before ascending to the summit of Stob Coire

# The Three Sisters

Sgreamhach. This fine outing is similar in parts to the Aonach Eagach (grade III). In descent, the easiest route is via the bealach at the head of the Lost Valley (NN 151 537), being very careful of the cornice and avalanche hazard.

The north face of Stob Coire Sgreamhach provides long and interesting approaches to the summit at around grade II, depending on the line you take. Walk up the Lost Valley path as far as the stream junction beyond the gorge (NN 154 543). From here, strike up the steepening slope to the south beneath the summit cone.

## Lost Valley Buttresses

| | |
|---|---|
| **Start** | Lay-by on the A82 at NN 171 568 |
| **Time** | 2hr 15min |
| **Crag base altitude** | 900m |
| **Route lengths** | 75–160m |
| **Route styles** | Turfy mixed climbing |
| **Avalanches** | Mainly in the descent routes |

It's a long walk to get to these buttresses but the turfy mixed climbing is excellent. Some of the best climbs in the area are found here, including Neanderthal.

### Approach
Walk south-east down onto the old road and follow this before finding a path leading to the bridge over the Coe. Use the metal steps and bridge, then follow the path into the Lost Valley (Coire Gabhail), through many boulders and crossing the stream, to emerge in its flat area. Follow the good path on the north-west side of the stream and its gorge before branching off right to the crags.

### Descent
Walk south-east to the col below Stob Coire Sgreamhach and descend north-east into the corrie. There's often a cornice, and the slope is steep at the start.

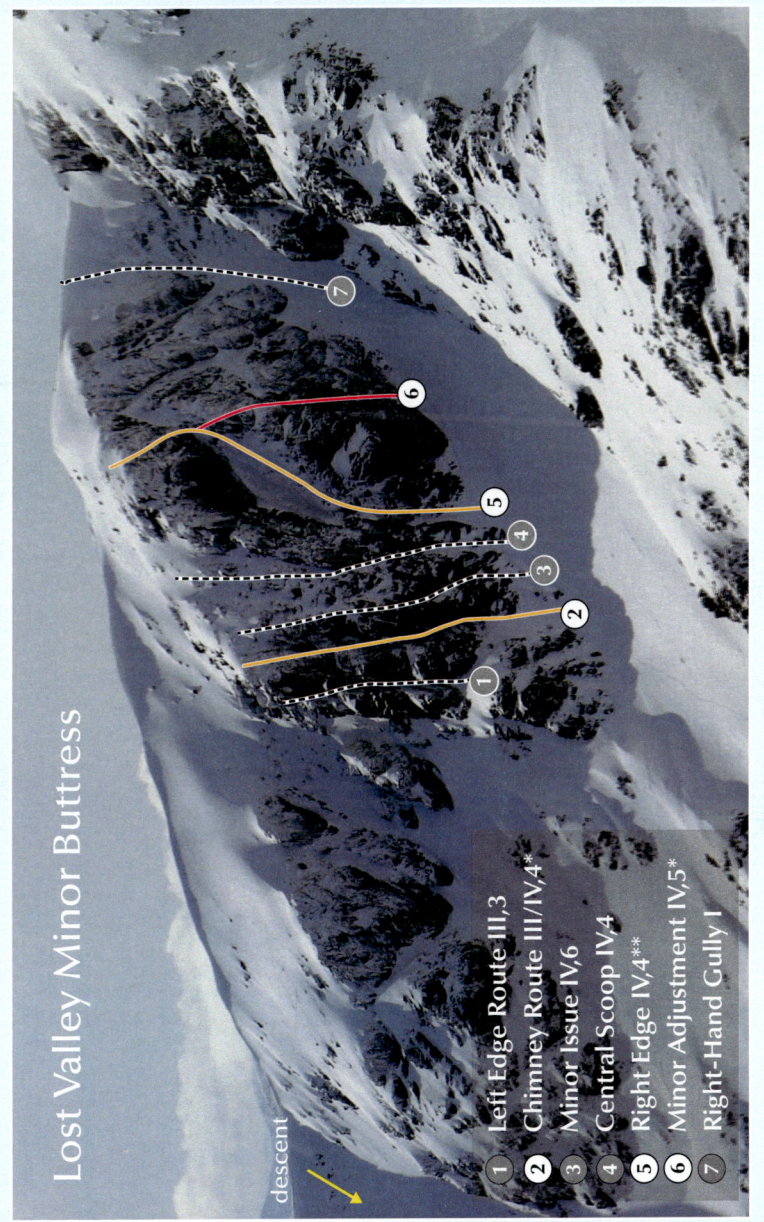

*Winter Climbs: Glen Coe*

## LOST VALLEY MINOR BUTTRESS NN 149 538

This is the smaller and left-hand of the two prominent buttresses at the head of the valley and below the middle of the ridge leading up from the col to Bidean nam Bian. Routes are described from left to right.

### Chimney Route 75m III/IV,4*
*R. Marshall and J. Moriarty, January 1959*
The obvious deep chimney to the left of the centre of the face. A series of chockstone pitches can give considerable difficulty.

### Right Edge 120m IV,4**
*J.R. Marshall, J. Stenhouse and D. Haston, February 1959*
At the right-hand side of the face, a broad snowfield ramp leads up rightwards below overhangs. Access to the ramp is gained by an icy chimney below its left end, and an arête leads from the top of the ramp to the summit.

### Minor Adjustment 115m IV,5*
*R. Anderson and C. Greaves, 19 February 1989*
The obvious groove and corner just up the gully from Right Edge; this is the direct line that joins that route after its upper traverse. Climb the groove steeply to a small ledge and spike, then go steeply left up a ramp around the edge to ledges. Traverse right back into the corner and belay higher up (45m). Climb the corner, move right and climb a short groove and step right below a small roof. Follow the snow ramp to a belay above a short wide crack (25m). Climb to the top (45m).

## LOST VALLEY BUTTRESS NN 148 540

The large right-hand buttress is in two distinct sections: an easier-angled left-hand portion, and a very steep portion set back at a higher level on the right. The routes are described from left to right. Neanderthal remains the most sought-after climb on the crag and very much worth the long walk.

### Sabre Tooth 135m IV,5*
*I. Clough and H. MacInnes, 9 February 1969*
Starting to the left of the corner, the route goes up into a recess and breaks out rightwards, eventually arriving on a terrace above the big corner. The corner can also be climbed at the same grade (**Delusion**). The terrace leads back left to the

# Lost Valley Buttress

1. Sabre Tooth IV,5*
2. Directosaur VI,7*
3. Pterodactyl V,6/7*
4. Moonlighting V,6*
5. Neanderthal VII,7***
6. Barracuda V,7**
7. Right-Hand Gully II

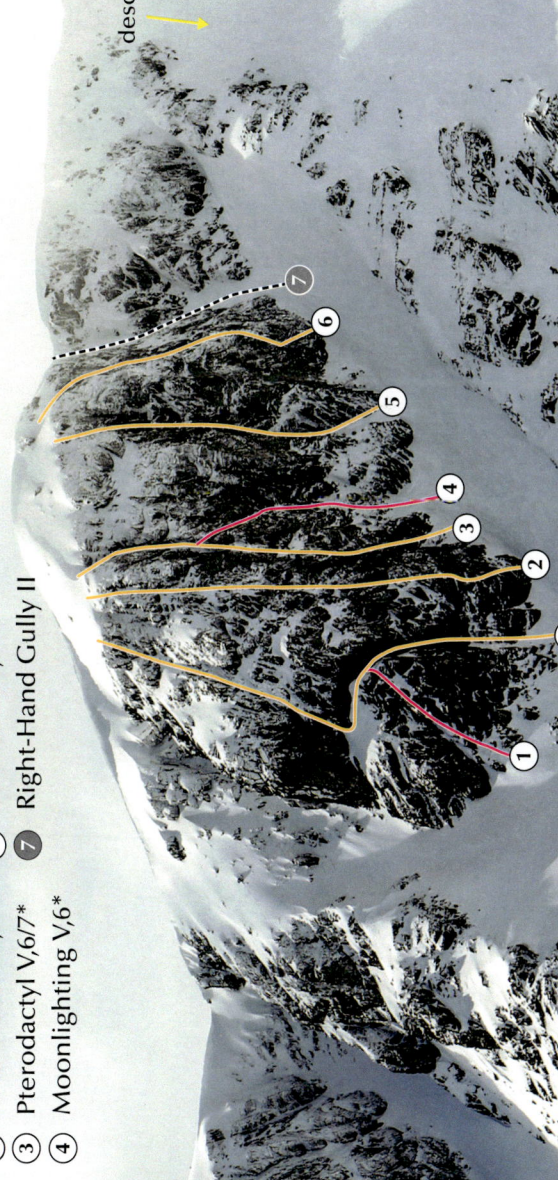

## Winter Climbs: Glen Coe

foot of a steep shallow 15m corner (good belays on the left). The corner is hard for a climb of this standard but well protected. Above it, a line of grooves is followed to the top.

### Directosaur 160m VI,7*

*G. Ettle, R. Anderson and R. Milne, March 1989*

Start at the lowest rocks and climb the serious shallow groove just left of the edge. Go left and up to a ledge which leads back right to the edge. Climb a steep flake-crack on the left and easier ground to below the corner of Tyrannosaur (45m). Climb the corner and grooves up the right side of a huge block-like feature to its top (30m). Go right and climb a short groove to regain the crest and snow grooves leading to the upper rocks and final slopes.

### Pterodactyl (Moonlight Gully) 110m V,6/7*

*H. MacInnes and D. Crabbe, January 1964*

This follows the line of the shallow gully lying in the corner, which divides the two sections of cliff. The overhanging entry to the upper couloir is difficult but

*Climbing Directosaur on Lost Valley Buttress*

relatively short. The route follows a steep corner to a stance beneath the overhang, which projects 2 metres, then climbs to gain the upper couloir using the crack to the left of the main icicle formation.

In years of good icing it may be possible to climb steep ice on the right of the central section. Chockstones have fallen out of this section.

### Moonlighting 120m V,6*
*R. Anderson, G. Taylor and N. West, 27 January 1988*
An obvious line right of Pterodactyl at the top of the bay. Gain the groove and a ledge at the foot of a wall (35m). Move up the steep flakeline on the left and go left at its top to the edge overlooking Pterodactyl, then move up right to a shallow groove which leads to a short wall (35m). Move into the gully of Pterodactyl, which is followed to the top (50m).

### Neanderthal 125m VII,7***
*R. Anderson and G. Nicholl, 14 February 1987*
An improbable-looking line up the huge corner, 30 metres right of Pterodactyl. Very good climbing according to those who've done it! Head easily up the gully and left wall to a platform, traverse right and climb the chute to a belay at a cul-de-sac (35m). Traverse right until it's possible to climb to the base of a corner and a small ledge (21m). Follow the corner to right side of a square roof. Move left underneath this and follow the recessed wall above towards an obvious narrow slot on the skyline (27m, belay). Easier climbing soon leads to the top.

### Barracuda 80m V,7**
*R. Anderson and R. Milne, January 1988*
Another steep and difficult mixed climb, although the easiest of the harder routes on this crag. It goes up the obvious steep crack-line which springs from the left-trending ramp-line right of Neanderthal. Start at the edge of the buttress and follow the ramp to a belay at the foot of the crack. Climb the crack (with very hard initial moves) to the buttress crest. Climb the gully above to the top.

## East face of Gearr Aonach

| | |
|---|---|
| **Start** | Lay-by on the A82 at NN 171 568 |
| **Time** | 1hr to the Lost Valley flats, plus between 15min and 1hr |
| **Crag base altitude** | 500m |
| **Route lengths** | 100–300m |
| **Route styles** | Turfy mixed climbing and cascade ice climbing |
| **Avalanches** | Exit slopes, gullies, and the descent into the Lost Valley can build wind slab. |

These climbs are all on the right-hand side of Coire Gabhail beyond the Lost Valley 10m boulder. They're particularly useful when conditions are poor at higher levels and for their relatively short approach. However, many of them are fine climbs in their own right, and some rank with the best in Glen Coe. Very icy conditions are preferable and the main ice climbs rarely form. In the stunning winters of the mid 1980s, huge curtains of ice built up all along the face. Such conditions have rarely been seen since, but ice does form here occasionally as it did in 2021. The gullies and mixed climbs might be in condition more often than expected.

### Approach

Walk south-east down onto the old road and follow this before finding a path leading to the bridge over the Coe. Use the metal steps and bridge, then follow the path into the Lost Valley (Coire Gabhail), through many boulders and crossing the stream, to emerge in the valley's flat area.

Try to work out the layout of the gullies before you cross the flats, as it's quite confusing when you're closer to them. Climbers new to the area should try and locate the more obvious gullies of Ingrid's Folly and Rev Ted's as useful reference points when exiting from the gorge section of the approach walk onto the flat area below the climbs.

For Lost Leeper Gully and Gullies A, B and C, follow the good path on the north-west side of the stream to the routes. For the Mome Rath Face routes, use the bottom section of Rev Ted's Gully and go slightly left to the terrace beneath the face.

## EAST FACE OF GEARR AONACH

**Descent**
The best descent is to walk towards Stob Coire nan Lochan and descend into the upper part of Coire nan Lochan or the Lost Valley, or by The Zig-Zags on the nose of Gearr Aonach if you know the route.

The routes are described from left to right.

### Gully C 230m I
*Probably Glencoe School of Winter Climbing (GSWC) parties*
A long shallow couloir on the extreme left before the cliffs fade out entirely. It may contain a few short pitches.

### Gully B 230m II
*Probably GSWC parties*
The next gully to the left of Gully A is straightforward except for one large chockstone pitch.

### Gully A 235m IV,4*
*H. MacInnes and D. Crabbe, January 1964*
Starting some distance beyond where the path rises from the floor of the Lost Valley. It runs the full height of the face, is indefinite in its lower part, deep-cut in the middle and becomes a steep straightforward slope in the upper section. It faces south and is hidden until you're immediately below it. A pitch climbed on the left leads into the gully, which is followed to the right to a bulging groove, the crux of the climb.

The Left Branch (IV,4) starts as a very steep ice pitch slightly to the left of the main Gully A. Follow the gully line throughout (escape possible halfway up on the left) and take either the chimney line above or break out right up steep iced rock. The Central Branch (IV) takes a line directly up a steep ice scoop from where Gully A divides at the start of the main pitch.

The next four climbs start on a big terrace, high up the face between Lost Leeper Gully and Rev Ted's Gully. Access to this terrace is difficult to find and is worth working out from the entrance to the Lost Valley before you cross the flats. The best way is to follow Rev Ted's Gully or turfy grooves and rocks to its left.

## Lost Leeper Gully 300m III,4**

*H. MacInnes, A. Gilbert, P. Debbage, D. Lane Joynt and D. Allwright, 13 February 1969*

The shallow indefinite gully that comes down immediately to the left of the Mome Rath Face and reaches the lower slopes of the valley above the gradually rising path. The route weaves its way up through the lower crags, giving interesting route-finding, and the more distinct upper gully should give at least two good ice pitches. The belays in the main part of the gully are poor.

## Rainmaker 100m VI,5**

*D. Cuthbertson and M. Duff, February 1980*
(no photo topo)

At the left-hand end of the upper face, next to Lost Leeper Gully, is a large ice-cased corner. Climb a long pitch up ice-smears to the left of the corner and belay in a recess. Now climb the corner with a short excursion on the left wall.

## Outgrabe Route 115m V,5**

*R. Anderson and R. Milne, January 1980*
(no photo topo)

A direct start and variation finish to Mome Rath Face Route, creating a virtually independent line. Start 10 metres left of Mome Rath Face Route and climb directly on steep turfy ground to a gully/chimney fault which is climbed in two pitches.

## Mome Rath Face Route 135m V,5***

*A. Fyffe and J. McArtney, 16 February 1969*

Combines sustained technical climbing with a high degree of exposure. The general line of the route is a long leftward slant. It starts below the icicle-fringed overhang by an obvious broad ramp and continues the line up to the left into a chimney. This is followed for about 20m before going left again into another chimney which leads to a bay. A slabby ice-plated rib on the left is followed by a short steep corner chimney.

## The Wabe 135m V,5***

*I. Clough, H. MacInnes and J. Hardie, 16 February 1969*
(no photo topo)

Another that is sustained throughout and extremely exposed, it approximately follows the line of a prominent icefall to the right of the icicle fringe. A short wall is climbed. Belay on a snow ledge above the main terrace. The route then goes up slightly to the right before making a long diagonal leftward traverse across the icefall towards a prominent nose and a stance at 45m.

After passing below the nose (immediately above an overhang) the route veers right then left to reach a pedestal stance below the right edge of the icicle fringe. Then move back right to climb the icefall where it passes through a recessed panel; there's a good stance on the right above this section. The final pitch goes diagonally right and then back left.

### Rev Ted's Gully 300m III*
*H. MacInnes and Rev Ted, February 1960*
Follows the obvious long couloir that slants leftwards up the full length of the face. The lower pitches are usually straightforward and lead to an obvious junction in the upper cliffs. Several alternatives are available. The best is to follow an ice-chimney line just to the left of the icefall at the junction or to take the icefall direct. If the easy right branch is followed, another steep chimney line will be found leading up from a bay – interesting but awkward. From the same bay an easy escape right can be made, reducing the whole climb to grade I/II.

> Between Rev Ted's and Ingrid's Folly and Peregrine Gully, the cliffs of Gearr Aonach give broken crags in the lower half leading to an almost continuous wide horizontal terrace. Above the terrace are a series of steep walls, unpleasantly grassy in summer, but which give good winter climbing. The first big break in these upper cliffs is a large rightward-facing corner – McArtney Gully III.

### Ingrid's Folly and Peregrine Gully 300m III*
*GSWC party*
The foot of Ingrid's Folly is only about a 5min walk diagonally up the slope to the west of the Lost Valley 10m boulder. It's a well-defined gully tucked away in a corner, and is much better than its appearance might suggest. The long grassy buttress to its right is John Gray's Buttress, grade II.

Ingrid's Folly consists of several relatively easy rock pitches which give good sport when veneered in ice. Above the last pitch, where the gully gives an easy slope to the top, a traverse to the left leads into Peregrine Gully. This gives further pitches; another cave with a through-route and an easy passage below a gigantic block which forms an archway just before the steep exit.

> The following climb lies on the area left of the imposing rock nose of Gearr Aonach that faces the road. It has the attraction of a short approach and quick descent.

### The Zig-Zags 200m II**

A popular route up the left side of the steep north face of Gearr Aonach that can be used as an approach to Stob Coire nan Lochan.

After crossing the bridge below the Meeting of Three Waters (NN 173 561) and following the track up towards Coire Gabhail (the Lost Valley) as far as the beginning of the gorge section (about 500 metres above the bridge), the route cuts up to the right, aiming for the cliffs of the east face of Gearr Aonach some distance to the left of the Nose. Although marked by occasional cairns, the route is not too easy to follow and it's wise to try and pick it out from well below.

Ancient geology has created two obvious slanting terraces, up to the right and then back to the left, winding up through otherwise sheer cliffs. The Zig-Zags is gained by walking leftwards up a grass slope below the cliffs until the start of the first terrace is reached in a corner immediately to the right of a 15m prow of rock. After about 30m of scrambling the terrace leads gently up to the right under some steep cliffs to an easy slope.

A series of short corners provide the crux and lead to a second big terrace, which is followed to its left-hand end. After a short climb, another long rightward-rising traverse and a brief tack back to the left lead to the top of the Nose of Gearr Aonach. The ridge is then followed until an easy traverse can be made into the floor of Coire nan Lochan.

Zig-Zags Direct (150m) cuts off a zig-zag at grade III. From the end of the first right-trending rake of The Zig-Zags, continue around the corner for a short distance (5m) until it's possible to climb the walls above. The first pitch (50m) leads to a good belay on a large ledge overlooking The Zig-Zags. Follow a hidden chimney up to the left, then scrappy ground to regain The Zig-Zags.

> In descent from Gearr Aonach, The Zig-Zags is difficult to find. Without prior knowledge, and certainly in poor visibility, the descent into Coire nan Lochan should be made.

# COIRE NAN LOCHAN

*North-west face of Gearr Aonach*

| | |
|---|---|
| **Start** | Lower lay-by on the A82 at NN 168 569 |
| **Time** | 1hr 30min |
| **Crag base altitude** | 650m |
| **Route lengths** | 85–300m |
| **Route styles** | Turfy mixed climbing and cascade ice climbing |
| **Avalanches** | Despite the gully name, avalanches are not common here. |

The huge north face of Gearr Aonach is the middle of the Three Sisters and dominates the view from Glen Coe. The Zig-Zags (described above) finds a line up the left side, and Avalanche Gully lies to the right side of this face, easily reached from the path used on the approach to Stob Coire nan Lochan.

### Approach
Walk straight down the slope to find the path that crosses the Coe at the wooden bridge. Follow the well-made path south-west into Coire nan Lochan. The path crosses a stream at an altitude of 200m; this stream leads into Avalanche Gully.

After an hour from the lay-by, the path goes underneath a natural overhang with a small shelter and past an awkward step. The stream crossed at this point leads to Rescue Team Gully and 999, but it's better to continue up the path to an obvious flattening at 570m and making a rising traverse back left to the crag.

### Descent
Descend The Zig-Zags if you know the route, or walk south-west and descend into Coire nan Lochan to the north.

## Avalanche Gully 300m IV,4*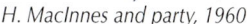
*H. MacInnes and party, 1960*
After crossing the bridge over the Coe, the main path strikes up towards the north face of Gearr Aonach before veering up to the right. The stream coming out of this

# STOB COIRE NAN LOCHAN

gully crosses the path at this point. In very cold weather, the lower part gives a series of short cascade ice pitches. The gully follows a rightward slant and leads to the summit of the Nose. Take the right forks at the lower and upper branches. The lower left branch is short, steep and interesting (grade IV). The upper left fork when in condition is grade IV.

The following two climbs are on the buttress below the highest point of the Gearr Aonach ridge on its east side. Although short, they have the attraction of easy access. They comprise various finishes to the approach gully and are described from left to right.

### Rescue Team Gully 85m II/III*
*H. MacInnes and party, March 1966*
The left-hand branch is a steep icy chimney with a through-route chockstone at its foot. Two good pitches.

### 999 135m IV,5**
*H. MacInnes and party, February 1969*
The right-hand branch gives a series of enjoyable short steep pitches in caves and up chimneys, finishing in a steep chockstone capped corner. A very good freeze is required to make essential turf solid. The right-trending line gives easier climbing.

*Stob Coire nan Lochan*
*1115m (NN 148 548)*

| | |
|---|---|
| **Start** | Lower lay-by on the A82, at NN 168 569 |
| **Time** | 2hr |
| **Crag base altitude** | 900m |
| **Route lengths** | 60–210m |
| **Route styles** | Excellent mixed climbing and some ice climbing |
| **Avalanches** | Cornices often build at the tops of the crags and gullies, and avalanches are quite common in the gullies and approach slopes. |

## Stob Coire nan Lochan

This magnificent peak dominates the view between Aonach Dubh and Gearr Aonach. It is best seen to the south-west from the lower lay-by on the A82, from where all approaches can start.

The cliffs high in the north-east-facing corrie immediately below the summit of Stob Coire nan Lochan usually give good winter climbing even when lower-level cliffs are spoiled by thaw. The floor of the corrie is at about 800m, and the cliffs, which have an average height of 165m, are arranged in a semicircle below the summit and the shoulder extending northwards from it.

The topography of the corrie is relatively simple. Below the summit of Stob Coire nan Lochan is Summit Buttress. This name applies particularly to the steep right-hand face; the open face and broken rocks of the left flank can be climbed anywhere at grade I standard. To the right of Summit Buttress are Broad Gully and Forked Gully, with Dorsal Arête in between. To the right again are the South, Central, North and Pinnacle buttresses, all separated by narrow gullies. Additionally, to the right of Pinnacle Buttress are some short gullies and rocky outcrops, not described below, which can provide good practice on a short day.

### Approach
Walk straight down the slope to find the path that crosses the Coe at the wooden bridge. Follow the well-made path south-west; a long, steady ascent up the valley eventually leads over the final lip to the floor of Coire nan Lochan (2hr). The path splits at a stream junction at a triangular boulder at 620m; cross the stream and go west then south-west up a final slope into the corrie.

Other possible approaches are via The Zig-Zags (described above), or by Dinner-Time Buttress or another climb on the west face of Aonach Dubh (described below).

### Descent
Descend north over the tops of the buttress, taking care to avoid the in-cut gullies and the cornices and going far enough to pass all the buttresses, before walking easily back into the corrie. If snow conditions are good, descend Broad Gully.

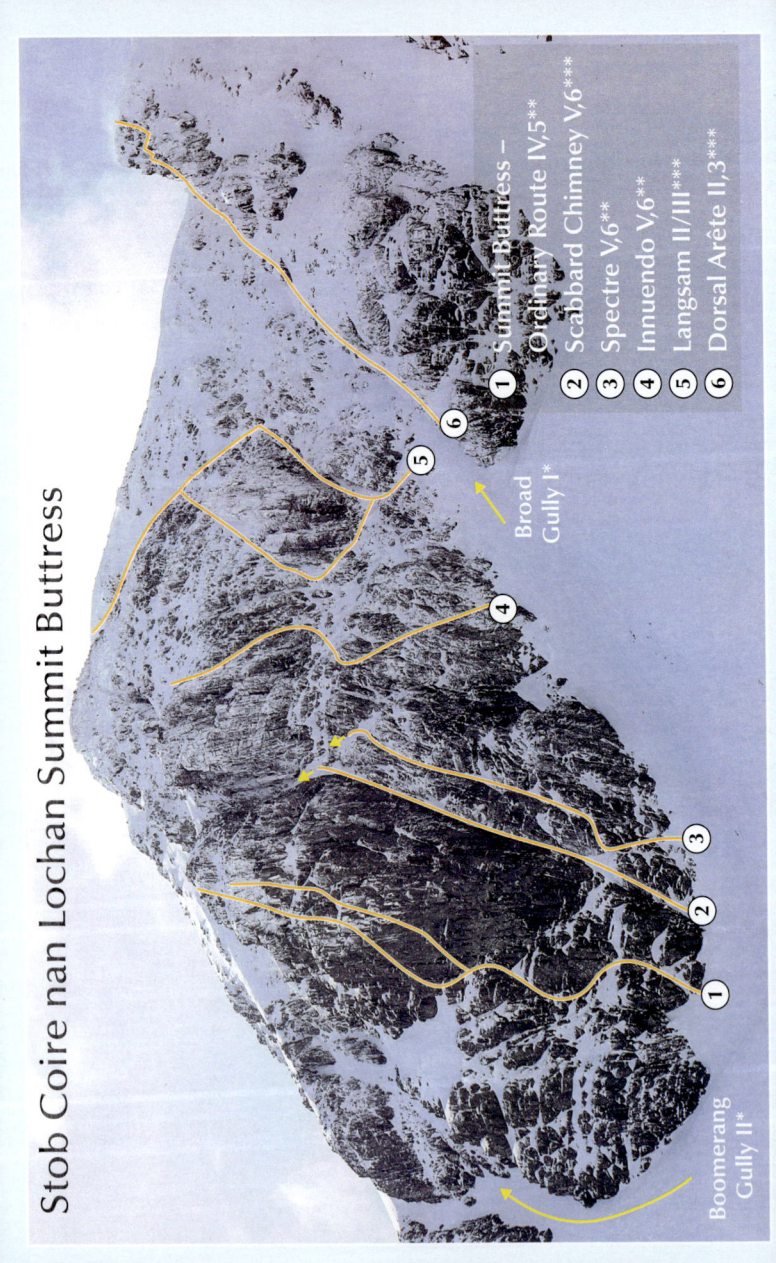

*Walking up to Stob Coire nan Lochan*

## Boomerang Gully 210m II*

*J. Black, R.G. Donaldson and W.H. Murray, January 1949*

This route curls round to the left of the steep rocks of Summit Buttress (and right of an indefinite rocky ridge which bounds the left flank) and swings back to finish by the ridge leading on from the top of the buttress to the summit of the mountain.

The first long tapering gully slope is followed up to the left from the foot of the steep rocks until an entry pitch on the right, rocky and frequently iced, leads up into the main couloir. If the entry pitch is missed the initial slope leads out onto the face of the left flank. The main couloir curves rightwards and leads to the final rocky arête.

## Ordinary Route 130m IV,5**

*K. Spence and party, February 1971*

Start just left of Scabbard Chimney and climb direct to a snow shelf then left to a corner. Follow the corner past a block and a snow shelf up left beneath the main buttress. An escape is possible into Boomerang Gully at this point. Ascend to the long, right-trending groove-and-crack system and stepped ledges to the top.

A harder variant (V,6**) is possible from the point where an escape can be made into Boomerang Gully by climbing an awkward short wall on the right which leads to a ledge system. Traverse the ledges rightwards, including a mantelshelf to a higher step and sensational block belay. Sustained climbing up the tapering groove above, then a short ramp and chimney, leads back left to easier ground (*M. Duff, N. Kekus, A. Nisbet, 7 January 1986*).

## WINTER CLIMBS: GLEN COE

### The Dual 133m IX,9***

*D. Cuthbertson and R. Anderson, 24 February 1999*
(no photo topo)
A modern test-piece of the highest order. Climb up from the right of Scabbard Chimney, which is crossed to gain a ramp which leads to a block belay (30m). Clip the poor in-situ gear up on the left before going back down to the foot of the wall, which is climbed up right to a break at the overhangs. Ascend the corner and move right (ignore peg/krab) to the edge, which is climbed up and around to the foot of the upper ramp (40m). Climb the ramp and wide crack to a chimney and terrace above. Large gear is useful on this pitch (35m). Climb the left-hand of three corners to easier ground (25m).

### Scabbard Chimney 120m V,6*** or

*L.S. Lovat, J.R. Marshall and A.H. Hendry, 12 February 1956*
The obvious chimney starting near the lowest rocks of the steep Summit Buttress and slanting up to the right. The crux is a 'sentry box' at about 65m. Above the chimney, a gully on the left leads up to the final arête. This route can be climbed as a rocky mixed route, but a good plating of snow and ice sometimes forms which can turn it into a near-continuous ice climb and make it a grade easier.

*Very icy mixed climbing on Scabbard Chimney and Spectre*

## Stob Coire nan Lochan

From the top of the hard section of this climb and the next, it is common to abseil from a good block down the steep wall (The Tempest X,9) to the right to the foot of Broad Gully.

### Spectre 120m V,6** or
*K. Bryan and J. Simpson, 12 January 1958*
Follows a steep shelf 12 metres right of Scabbard Chimney. Climb Scabbard Chimney and traverse right across slabs from the foot of its first chimney to a point where an awkward descent gains the long shelf. Alternatively, climb directly into the shelf line. Climb an icy bulge and groove followed by a steep slab and bulge to easier ground. Continue to a broad ledge and the narrow gully of Scabbard Chimney. As with Scabbard Chimney, this route forms a good amount of ice and is better for it.

### Innuendo 150m V,6**
*H. MacInnes, R. Birch, P. Judge and R. O'Shea, 1969*
Starts above Broad Gully, opposite and level with the foot of Dorsal Arête, below an obvious chimney groove that leads to a ledge cutting across the face. Climb the chimney groove past a ledge (36m) into an overhung bay. Exit by an awkward chimney on the right and ascend more easily rightwards to a block belay below the upper wall. Traverse right beneath an overhung chimney until it's possible to climb steep cracks and gain the chimney by moving left above the overhanging section. Follow more easily up the chimney to the top.

### Langsam 200m II/III***
*H. MacInnes, M.C. MacInnes and party, March 1969*
Starts up the gully from Innuendo and follows the snow slope until under a rock wall. Then, either: traverse left on steep snow and up right to a short gully and the top; or climb a chimney on the right under the wall and continue the traverse up left to steeper snow then easier ground.

### Broad Gully 150m I*
A very easy route which often provides the best means of descent into the corrie and rarely forms a cornice, but care may be required in icy conditions.

### Dorsal Arête 120m II,3***
*J. Black, T. Shepherd, J. Allingham and J. Bradburn, 28 January 1951*
Start a few metres up Broad Gully and climb the arête on its right. The route becomes increasingly interesting as height is gained, finally tapering to a very narrow and well-defined arête which should be climbed directly on the crest but can

be bypassed on the left. There are good rock belays, but the blocks can be a little loose on the arête, after which the route goes either up right by a snowy ramp or left into a steep groove in the final buttress (III).

The climb is very useful in bad conditions and many harder direct starts are possible on the lower front face of the buttress between Broad and Forked gullies.

### Forked Gully 135m I/II*

The gully to the right of Dorsal Arête, giving a steep but normally straightforward snow climb by the Left Fork. The Right Fork (right of the 60m rock rib that splits the upper section) is steeper (II/III) and more often icy.

### Twisting Grooves 130m IV,5**

*W. Sproul and T. Carruthers, 11 March 1962*

Starts 30 metres to the left of Twisting Gully and follows a line of corners. Ascend the first corner to a small snow patch and continue up a crack topped by an overhanging chockstone (25m). Continue to a snow patch above the first pitch of Twisting Gully (30m) followed by snow to the bottom of a chimney (55m). The chimney leads to broken rocks near the top (20m).

### Twisting Gully 150m III,4**

*W.H. Murray, D. Scott and J.C. Simpson, December 1946*

One of the classic Scottish snow climbs, although the interesting sections are short lived. This route takes a shallow gully immediately to the left of South Buttress and is separated from Forked Gully by an indefinite rocky rib. The first 30m leads up

*Climbing Twisting Grooves*

into a deep recess from which there are two continuations. The normal route follows an icy chimney on the left until it bulges, where a short left traverse is made across the gully wall to gain the left rib. The Right Fork (IV,5**) climbs an ice corner on the right and the continuation runnel.

There's an awkward mantelshelf move on the short arête which leads to easier ground. Above this crux pitch, about 30m of snow leads to another short ice pitch which can be turned on the right if necessary. The gully continues without difficulty to the final wide fan and a choice of steep exits.

## Moonshadow 150m IV,5**

*K. Crocket and C. Stead, January 1972*
An interesting finish to the Right Fork of Twisting Gully. From the ice corner above the first main pitch of that route, climb the right wall to a belay in a corner (35m). Climb the chimney past a chockstone and more steep rocks to the top.

## Chimney Route 125m VI,6***

*First ascent unknown*
A good route which benefits from some ice. Start opposite the foot of Twisting Gully at the left end of a snow ledge. Climb steeply up the chimney (25m) then continue and go slightly right up turf to the left end of the upper terrace (45m). As for Tilt, a wall and a V-groove lead to the crest (25m), then easier climbing to the top (30m).

A variant is possible on pitch 2 by going straight up into the wide chimney above. This is separated from the upper terrace by a huge fin of rock.

## Tilt 140m VI,7***

*M. Hamilton, K. Spence and A. Taylor, January 1980*
A steep mixed climb with little ice and reasonable protection. This climb follows a very prominent chimney line just left of the blunt buttress crest. Follow cracks to the obvious chimney and groove (40m). Climb the groove until you're above an overhang. Move right with difficulty and climb a wall to belay on a large flake, or continue by following more grooves (delicate) to a terrace. Finish by a chimney and obvious V-groove on the left.

## Unicorn 125m VIII,8***

*C. MacLean and A. Nisbet, 24 January 1985; FFA C. Smith and L. Collier, February 1999*
The obvious corner gives a sustained and outstanding climb. Three pitches lead to a shattered ledge, from where a fourth pitch up a chimney then the wall on the right are climbed to gain the top.

## SC Gully 150m III,3***

*P.D. Baird, L. Clinton and F. Clinton, March 1934*

The steep gully between South and Central buttresses is another classic and a serious route requiring good snow-ice conditions. Early in the season a steep ice pitch often bars entry to the gully; if it's too formidable, the rib on the left may give an easier alternative. Steep snow then leads up into the bed of the gully proper. The route then traverses up to the right to gain and follow a steep ice gangway which often has a bulge shortly before the top. A long pitch will normally be required to reach a satisfactory belay. Beyond this, steep snow leads to the cornice, which may be quite difficult.

## East Face Route 130m VI,7**

*M. Hamilton and R. Anderson, 20 March 1982*

On the east face of Central Buttress overlooking SC Gully are two parallel chimney systems. This route climbs partway up the left-hand one before moving into the chimney on the right.

Climb the chimney and move left onto a pedestal (20m), then go back right and climb past the left end of a roof in the corner to belay in a shallow recess (15m). Gain the right-hand chimney system by difficult moves across the wall, around the arête, then up and right (30m). Follow the steep chimney to a belay on its left wall (45m). Go right to the crest and the finish of Raeburn's Route (20m).

The left-hand chimney may be climbed in its entirety including the clean-cut corner crack in the headwall to give a very sustained icy mixed route – possibly one of the best of its type in Scotland (**East Face Direct Direct VII,8** *P. Benson and G. Robertson*).

## Central Grooves 120m VII,7***

*K. Spence and J. McKenzie, February 1983*

A well-protected, hard mixed route. More difficult than Tilt by being more sustained. To the right of SC Gully is Central Buttress; the climb starts at the lowest rocks and follows an obvious groove just left of the crest throughout. The first section takes longer to rime up than the rest of the crag.

## Central Buttress 135m VII,7***

*K. Spence and M. Hamilton, 12 February 1981*

From a distance, an elongated S-shaped crack can be seen starting from the foot of the buttress. This is the route. Follow Central Grooves pitch 1 (30m), then traverse right, climbing the wall to a corner which is followed to a ledge on the crest (20m). A short wall above is followed by easier ground rightwards to the edge. Go

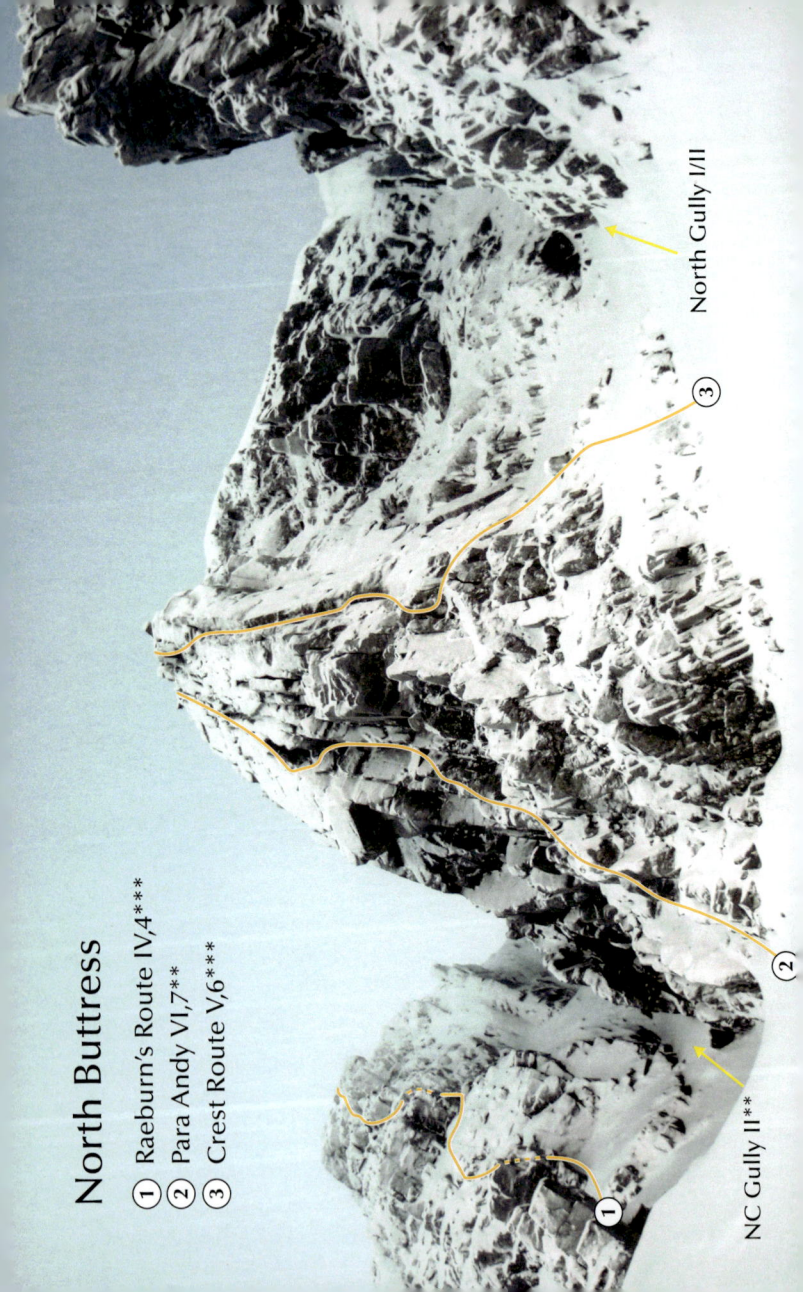

right and climb a pinnacle to a small snowfield (40m). Follow the chimney above before breaking out right below the top, and climb the last part of Raeburn's Route (45m).

### Raeburn's Route 150m IV,4***
*H. Raeburn with Dr and Mrs C. Inglis Clark, April 1907*
A good route with excellent situations. Starts from the bay to the left of the lowest right-hand spur and goes up a chimney to the right to gain the crest of the spur on the right. The ridge leads to a tower, which is best turned on the right, regaining the crest by a short chimney and climbing up grooves to another tower. Turn this on the right as well, move back left to the crest and follow this to the top.

Note: it's possible to bypass the initial long pitch by a traverse from the lower reaches of NC Gully. The first pitch is, however, very good!

### NC Gully 155m II**
The gully between Central and North buttresses generally gives a steep but straightforward snow climb. Early in the season it may have a short pitch of rocky mixed ground. A good introductory gully.

On the right wall of NC Gully is an obvious tower with a roof at half-height which helps in locating the following three climbs.

### Evening Citizen 95m V,7**
*K. Spence, H. MacInnes and A. Thompson, 1971*
(no photo topo)
Left of the roofed tower is a well-defined corner/chimney which gives the route to the crest.

### Para Andy 90m VI,7**
*A Cunningham, A. Nesbit and A. Newton, 8 January 1988*
Climb the big corner/groove right of the roofed pillar. Climb direct to the groove (35m). Climb the groove until tight against a roof (loose), and traverse left to a mantelshelf. There's a belay ledge on the front face above the roof. Pass the short wall above to the left and back right to a crack-line in the centre of the face, which is climbed until it's possible to move left to a ledge and blocky arête leading to the top.

## Intruder 100m V,7**

*R. Anderson and G. Nicoll, 14 February 1988*
(no photo topo)

Climbs the slimmer right-hand groove right of the tower, starting at the lowest rocks. Go up left, to the bottom of the groove (15m). Ascend the groove with difficulty, passing two pegs to a flake, and continue to a ledge beneath the flake of Financial Times (25m). Gain the groove on the left and climb it to the top of a pinnacle. Go up, then right to climb a short groove, then right to belay by a perched block (35m). Easy to the top (25m).

## Crest Route 115m V,6***

*R. Anderson and M. Hamilton, 24 November 1985*

To the right of NC Gully is North Buttress. This climb, well protected and sustained, follows an obvious groove just right of the buttress crest and starts at the lowest rocks. Climb broken stepped ground, a short wall and cracks to belay on a pedestal (35m). Climb a flake-crack above, and move right across a slab to gain a corner which is followed to the crest. Step left at a large spike onto a ledge (30m). Follow the groove above to a shelf with a short wall that is overcome by a stepped flake-crack on the right. Belay at a prominent flat boulder with a good thread.

*Ideal conditions for rocky mixed climbing on Crest Route*

*Climbing Crest Route*

### North Gully 75m I/II
Divides North Buttress and Pinnacle Buttress. This climb is steep, sometimes gives a short pitch and often carries a heavy cornice.

### Pinnacle Buttress Groove 60m III*
*L.S. Lovat and N.G. Harthill, 5 January 1958*
(no photo topo)
An excellent short climb in icy conditions. Follows a steep groove on the North Gully flank of Pinnacle Buttress to the left of a prominent arête. Start on the right near the foot of North Gully.

## AONACH DUBH EAST FACE

On the opposite side of the stream to the Stob Coire nan Lochan approach path is a huge area of steep rock forming many buttresses. In very cold weather some cascade ice climbs form among these buttresses, offering a variety of good short climbs. Low on the right of the face is Lady Jane Wall. Higher up and to the left are Weeping Wall and Barn Wall. Left again is a small hanging corrie with Far Eastern Buttress on its left.

## Far Eastern Buttress

| | |
|---|---|
| Start | Lower lay-by on the A82 at NN 168 569 |
| Time | 1hr 45min |
| Crag base altitude | 650m |
| Route lengths | 70–120m |
| Route styles | Turfy mixed climbing |
| Avalanches | Rarely a problem on the crag |

These routes are best approached from the stream crossing at the triangular boulder on the Stob Coire nan Lochan path and a traverse right to the foot of the buttress from this point. The climbs are all mixed routes requiring a good freeze and frozen turf with some ice.

### Approach
Walk straight down the slope to find the path that crosses the Coe at the wooden bridge. Follow the well-made path south-west into Coire nan Lochan. The path splits at the stream junction at 620m; cross the stream and traverse right to the foot of the buttress.

### Descent
Walk left from the top of the crag to descend south back to the foot of the crag.

### Orient Express 85m IV,5*
*R. Anderson, C. Anderson and R. Milne, 2 February 1991*
The thin chimney in the middle of the face just left of the more obvious corner of Eastern Slant. Climb straight up on ice to the belay of Eastern Slant (40m). Climb the steep chimney above and left (25m). Continue to a boulder at the top (20m).

### Eastern Slant 120m III,4*
*R. Anderson, C. Anderson and R. Milne, 16 February 1992*
The obvious, rising corner line. Climb the corner (40m) then follow the traverse line left around an edge, across a slab to a corner and belay on the left (40m). Continue in the same line to finish up a short chimney (40m).

# Far Eastern Buttress

1. Eastern Slant III,4*
2. Orient Express IV,5*
3. Nirvana Wall VI,8**
4. Yen VI,7

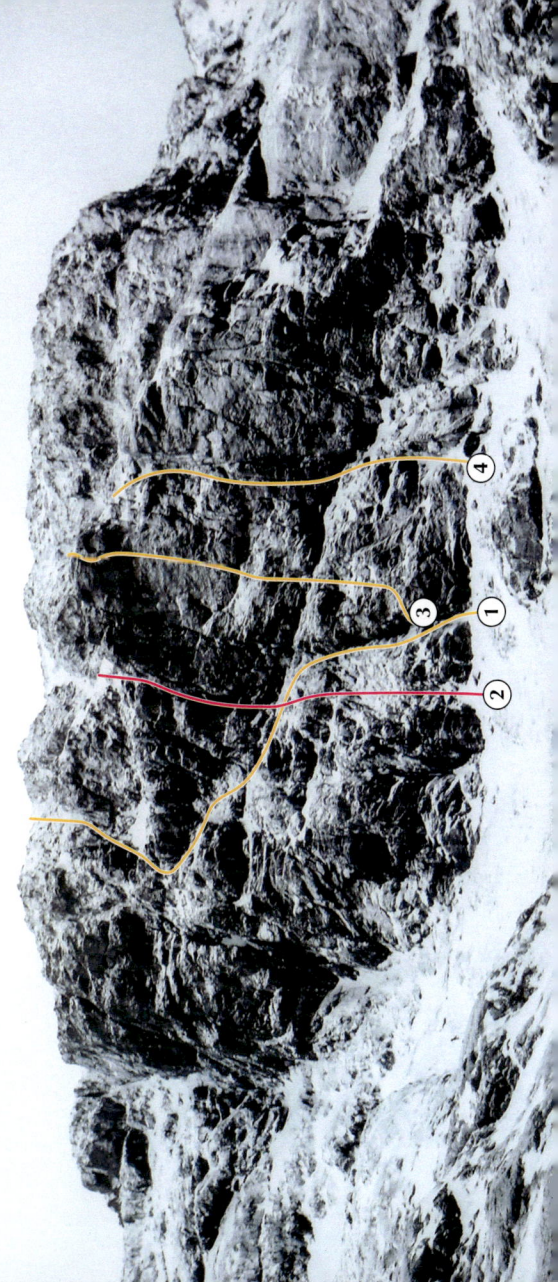

### Nirvana Wall 75m VI,8**

*D. King and M. Pescod, 21 December 2003*

Based on the summer line up the striking crack in the steep slab high on the buttress. Start up Eastern Slant and break out right to climb the front of the buttress to a ledge (35m). Continue up steep cracks to another good ledge (10m). Climb the crack with awkward moves at the top through a bulge (30m).

### Yen 70m VI,7

*R. Anderson and C. Anderson, 9 February 1991*

The cracks on the right of Nirvana Wall. Follow an obvious chimney and traverse up and left to a short corner (40m). The corner and cracks lead to a ledge (20m). Step left and continue up the groove (40m).

---

**LADY JANE WALL NN 159 562**

Very occasionally, ice climbs form on this wall. The last time was 2010. They are all steep and thin cascades with poor protection but a quick walk in. Approach is by the good path towards Stob Coire nan Lochan to where it heads steeply uphill. Follow the old path right to a huge boulder in the stream, cross the stream and reach the crag directly. There are four excellent routes climbed in 2010 plus Excellerator which forms a little more often.

---

### Exellerator 25m V,5*

*W. Todd, February 1986*

(no photo topo)

Often fatter than it looks, but it's also steeper than it looks.

### Jane's Weep 25m VIII,8*

*D. MacLeod and B. Fyffe, 13 January 2010*

(no photo topo)

'Ice smears a few millimetres thick and occasional blobs running boldly up a wall, eventually gaining thicker ice to finish on an overhanging pillar.' – Dave MacLeod describes what is probably the hardest pitch of ice climbing in Scotland.

## North face of Aonach Dubh

| | |
|---|---|
| **Start** | Lower lay-by on the A82 at NN 168 569 |
| **Time** | 1hr 30min |
| **Crag base altitude** | 500m |
| **Route lengths** | 125–370m |
| **Route styles** | Cascade ice climbing and mixed climbing |
| **Avalanches** | Not normally a problem |

Aonach Dubh's north face is dominated by the huge dark recess of Ossian's Cave. The cave itself is situated above a terrace, Sloping Shelf, which slants up from left to right and starts at the apex of the approach triangle. The right leg of this approach triangle is formed by a gully containing many waterfalls and lying to the left of the vegetated terrace walls which rise from the floor of the glen to Ossian's Cave. The left leg is a slanting grassy ramp topped by cliffs which are split by a huge Y-shaped gully, Ossian's Close. Cascade-style ice climbs form on either side of Ossian's Close, but to the left of Ossian's Cave, the climbs are mixed.

The path up the right side of the triangle is often icy, so the recommended approach is along the grassy ramp (as the climbs are described) after crossing the Coe as for the direct walk into Stob Coire nan Lochan.

To the left of Ossian's Close is a broad corridor which slants up right into the top of the gully. The icefall of Findlay's Rise starts at the foot of this corridor and rises on the left wall. The steep and grassy nature of the approaches to all of the climbs provides a potentially dangerous base for avalanches after heavy snowfalls or during thaw conditions.

### Approach
Walk straight down the slope to find the path that crosses the Coe at the wooden bridge. Instead of following the path, walk west, cross the streams and follow the big grassy ramp that leads directly to Ossian's Close.

### Descent
From the top, walk south into Coire nan Lochan and walk down the path in the corrie.

## North face of Aonach Dubh

### Darwin's Dihedral 240m VI,6**
*D. Cuthbertson and M. Lawrence, 28 December 1981*
Towards the left end of the cliffs is a Y-shaped feature, obvious from the road. Climb the icefall beneath and the large right-facing branch of the corner which is to the left of the gully of Venom. (Divergence (IV,4) climbs the left branch of Darwin's Dihedral, avoiding the crux of this route.) Take the buttress on the left of the ice to gain the higher basin and follow the deep chimney of the left branch.

### Venom 240m IV/V,5*
*A. McAllister, M. Duff, R. Anderson and D. Brown, January 1979*
Start about 30 metres left of Findlay's Rise below a steep chimney in the initial buttress. Climb the long chimney to trees and move left to gain and climb the gully left of White Snake. To the left of the initial pitch is a less obvious chimney which can be taken as a direct start to the main gully (**Viper Start IV,5***R. Anderson and D. Brown, February 1979*).

### White Snake 240m IV,4**
*R. Anderson, A. McAllister, D. Brown and M. Duff, January 1979*
Climb the icefall just to the left of Findlay's Rise to a cave formed by a huge block. Follow a left-slanting ramp then climb more easily up a gully to a roof. Traverse left to avoid the roof, regain the gully and continue to the top.

### Findlay's Rise 240m IV,5*
*I. Nicholson and party, 1978*
A fine cascade ice climb. Start at the icefall at the foot of the left wall of the corridor. Move steeply left onto the foot of the ice, and climb less steeply to a small cave and belay. A long pitch leads to the top of the icefall, from where mixed ground gives access to the summit.

### Ossian's Close 240m III*
*H. MacInnes and C. Williamson, February 1979*
Above and slightly to the left of the apex of the approach triangle is a huge Y-gully. This is an unusual route, and not as hard as it looks. Climb above the path to gain the gully at 15m. Easy ground leads to an ice wall going left to a cave. The upper section of the gully is gained by a through-route leading to an easy exit.

### Midnight Special 300m V,5*
*I. Clough and K. Spence, 1969*
The prominent depression to the left of Ossian's Cave, starting just up to the right from the apex of the approach triangle. From the bottom of the depression, climb

# Aonach Dubh North Face Right Side

1. Midnight Special V,5*
2. Midnight Cowboy V,6*
3. Against All Odds VI/VII,7**
4. Fingal's Chimney VI,7***
5. Fall Out VII,7***
6. Deep Gash Gully IV

a steep pitch (crux) to reach a shallow gully. Climb this and bear left to reach the summit slopes, or finish directly by the line of the depression.

### Midnight Cowboy 370m V,6**
*D. Knowles, Dud Knowles and W. Thomson, 1974*
Follows the line of an obvious gully running straight up, left of Shadbolt's Chimney which is the obvious chimney left of Ossian's Cave. Start midway between Shadbolt's Chimney and Midnight Special. Follow iced walls and a chimney into the deepening gully, which is followed with difficulty and poor protection to the top.

### Against All Odds 150m VI/VII,7**

*M. Fowler and C. Watts, 14 February 1988*

A prominent line right of Ossian's Cave and left of Fingal's Chimney. Start left of the weakness at a tree. Go up right and tension to a bendy sapling in the fault, then climb an overhang on turf tufts to a niche and exit right to climb up to a nut belay (30m). Climb a short wall on the right and the overhang above in the corner. Climb on tufts just right of the corner and gain a ramp coming in from the right, then continue to a belay ledge (30m).

Climb on minimal ice-smears and tufts right of the wide crack to beneath the overhanging section. On the first ascent, three pegs were used to reach the next tufts leading steeply to snow. Gain a belay below a snow-filled chimney which slants up left (30m). Keep going in line with the lower pitches on minimal tufts and ice and protection to easier ground and a snow slope which ends 15m below Pleasant Terrace (45m). Follow a ramp on the left to Pleasant Terrace (15m). Either descend Pleasant Terrace or take easy slopes on the left.

### Fingal's Chimney 190m VI,7***

*W. Tauber and D. Gardner, 1969*

A fine, sustained mixed climb requiring a lot of snow to be in good condition. One of the longest chimney climbs in the area, with very few ascents. Right of Ossian's Cave are two narrow chimneys cutting the big wall; Fingal's Chimney is the right-hand of these.

From the base of the chimney a series of ledges runs down rightwards, terminating by a pinnacle. Start at the pinnacle and climb its right edge. A delicate traverse left beneath overhangs is made to a ramp which leads to the base of the chimney (45m). Climb the chimney in three long pitches to Pleasant Terrace. Either continue easily up the chimney or traverse left into Midnight Cowboy, which can be followed to the top.

### Fall-Out 125m VII,7***

*G. Taylor and R. Anderson, 23 January 1988*

Start below the narrow chimney at the foot of Deep-Gash Gully and climb a corner and wall to belay just right of the chimney (30m). Climb the chimney to belay beneath a huge chockstone (25m), and continue up the chimney to a ledge (25m). Move right along the ledge to another chimney (possible belay), which is climbed to the foot of a short chimney/crack (40m). Move up then left to easier ground and back right to grooves, short walls and a ledge (40m). Continue up left to easier ground.

# COIRE NAM BEITHEACH

The magnificent northern corrie of Bidean nam Bian is contained in the horse-shoe ridges linking Aonach Dubh, Stob Coire nan Lochan, Bidean nam Bian, Stob Coire nam Beith and An-t-Sròn. Looking up into the corrie, the west face of Aonach Dubh is on the left, facing the Clachaig Inn and Glencoe village; Diamond Buttress and Church Door Buttress are on the north face of Bidean nam Bian and visible from the car park at Loch Achtriochtan; and the north-west-facing cliff of Bishop's Buttress is on the flank of the north spur of the west top of Bidean nam Bian, with the immense cliff of Stob Coire nam Beith leading directly to its summit.

All of the climbing areas in Coire nam Beitheach are complex places which take several visits to understand. The west face of Aonach Dubh and Stob Coire nam Beith in particular are huge, sprawling areas full of ridges and gullies, crossed by ledges and terraces. Piecing together the layout of these areas is a very satisfying process which provides the excuse to keep going back. Overlooking all of them is Church Door Buttress, which is always worth the longer walk in.

Climbing Number Six Gully on Aonach Dubh's west face

Coire nam Beitheach

The main approach for the corrie starts from Loch Achtriochtan; an efficient route follows the fence on the west side of Allt Coire nam Beithach all the way in.

## West face of Aonach Dubh

| | |
|---|---|
| **Start** | Car park at Loch Achtriochtan (NN 139 567) |
| **Time** | 1hr 30min |
| **Crag base altitude** | 550m |
| **Route lengths** | 75–600m |
| **Route styles** | Cascade ice climbing and mixed climbing |
| **Avalanches** | This is a big, complex face and cross loading normally occurs, creating avalanche hazards where you would not normally expect them. |

## Winter Climbs: Glen Coe

Aonach Dubh is the right-hand of the Three Sisters and its west face looks down onto the Clachaig Inn. It's a vast and complex series of buttresses and gullies. If the snow level is low, the face comes quickly into condition and so provides one of the more popular cliffs in the Glen.

The buttresses are split horizontally into three tiers by Middle Ledge, between the lowest and middle tiers, and The Rake, between the middle and upper tiers. Splitting the face vertically are six main gullies numbered from left to right, and there are two scoops which split the main mass of the middle tier.

### Approach

Walk past the cottage at Achnambeithach on the outside of the fence and follow the fence to the stream coming out of Number Two Gully in the west face of Aonach Dubh. To find Dinner-Time Buttress, go straight up the spur on the left side of the stream and Number Two Gully. To find B Buttress and The Screen, cross the stream and go straight up the spur on the right side of the stream and Number Two Gully. To find Number Six Gully, continue to follow bits of fence posts up underneath the west face of Aonach Dubh before climbing straight up into the gully.

An alternative approach starts through a gate immediately west of the road bridge spanning the River Coe. The path climbs steeply to the south (beware of an icy patch on the path) and after about 1hr levels off into a short gorge. At this point it's better to descend to the stream bed and follow either side of the stream in the gorge. Access to the west face of Aonach Dubh can be made from here.

### Descent

From the top, walk east into Coire nan Lochan, or traverse south-west into Coire nam Beitheach. It's also possible to descend the top part of Number Two Gully before moving out onto the lower part of Dinner-Time Buttress – a route that's tricky to find if you don't know it.

### Dinner-Time Buttress 335m II**

Lies on the left-hand side of the face below the col between Aonach Dubh and Stob Coire nan Lochan. It's defined by the vague Number One Gully on the left and by the deep watercourse of Number Two Gully on the right. Except for the

*High on the west face of Aonach Dubh*

final section, it's mainly grass with short sections of scrambling. Can be used to approach the climbs on Stob Coire nan Lochan. A good bad-weather route.

Various options can be found on reaching the final rocky section, and all are worthwhile:
- traverse left into Number One Gully (grade I/II);
- climb a short awkward chimney in the frontal face of the buttress between Number One and Two gullies; followed by some interesting scrambling (grade II);
- traverse right into Number Two Gully by a rising shelf (grade I); or
- climb an icy gully up left at the point where Number Two Gully is entered (grade II).

The following two routes are on the north face of B Buttress overlooking Number Two Gully.

### Middle Ledge 600m II
(no photo topo)
Gained from Number Two Gully, the ledge gives an exposed if easy traverse. The only difficulty lies in the initial pitch out of Number Two Gully. On reaching Number Four Gully, ascend the middle section of the gully without difficulty and escape left along The Rake. Impressive scenery.

### Cyclops 105m IV,5*
*H. MacInnes and party, January 1970*
(no photo topo)
At the start of Middle Ledge a steep corner goes directly up B Buttress. Climb this to easier ground. Take the chimney line above to gain an eye in the buttress. From the other side of the eye, climb rocks to the top.

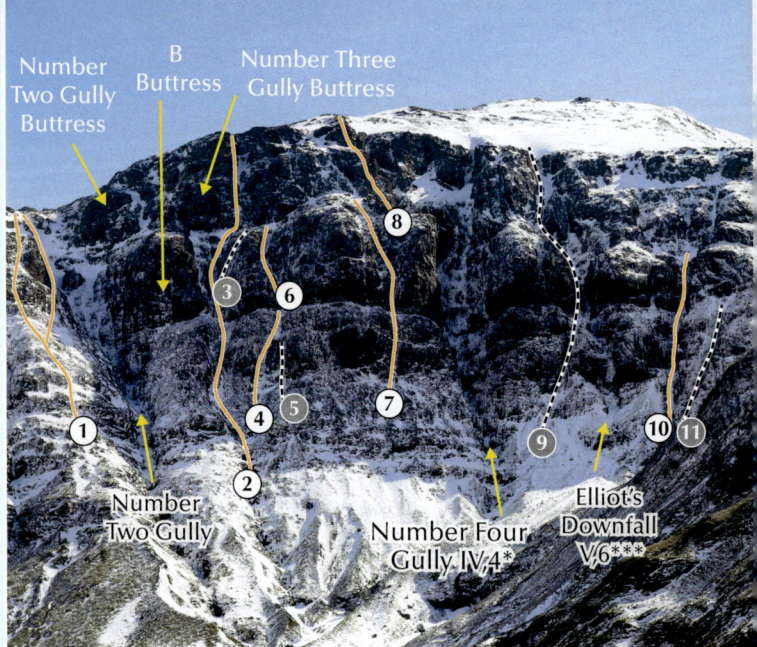

## Aonach Dubh West Face

1. Dinner-Time Buttress II**
2. Number Three Gully III***
3. The Smear IV,4*
4. The Screen IV,5*
5. The Flute V,5*
6. C-D Scoop II**
7. Amphitheatre Scoop Direct V,5***
8. Amphitheatre North Ridge
9. Number Five Gully III*
10. Number Six Gully IV,4***
11. Chaos Chimney III*

## West face of Aonach Dubh

### The Pinnacle Face 110m IV,5*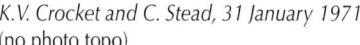
*K.V. Crocket and C. Stead, 31 January 1971*
(no photo topo)
Climb the obvious chimney just right of the groove of Cyclops. Take care with a large block resting on a slab halfway up. From the top of the chimney, climb rightwards and up to the right edge of the buttress at a small pinnacle. A steep wall is climbed on the right to the easier ground, past the eye of Cyclops and on up to The Rake above.

> Above The Rake and looking down Number Two Gully is Number Two Gully Buttress. A few excellent turfy mixed routes are found here, such as Rose Late (IV,6), Oz (VII,7) and The Wonderful Wizard (V,6).
>
> Above The Rake and looking straight down Number Three Gully is Number Three Gully Buttress. A few good rocky mixed climbs are found here, such as R2D2 (V,6), C3PO (V,6) and H5N8 (IV,5) which climb to the top of the two-tier buttress in four pitches.

### Number Three Gully 300m III***
*Crofton and Evans, March 1934*
This gully immediately right of B Buttress is shallow and rather indefinite except where it cuts through the middle tier. Often giving a good ice pitch at the start, it can also bank out and become easier. The top part, often avoided by The Rake, is well worth doing. The Smear (75m IV,4*) is the icefall that lies on the right wall of Number Three Gully where it cuts the middle tier and is a pleasant climb which can provide a suitable continuation to The Screen.

### The Screen 75m IV,5*
*D. Bathgate and J. Brumfitt, February 1965*
The obvious large icefall that forms over the lowest tier of rocks to the right of Number Three Gully. Climb for 25m to an icicle recess, step left and move up to rock belays on the left. Trend right to Middle Ledge. An enjoyable route. Just to the right of The Screen is a narrow icy chimney, The Flute (V,5*).

### C-D Scoop 150m II**
*D. Bathgate and J. Brumfitt, February 1965*
The easy gully splitting the middle tier above The Screen.

# Aonach Dubh West Face (right side)

Elliot's Downfall V,6***

1. Amphitheatre Scoop Direct V,5***
2. Number Four Gully IV,4*
3. Southern Death Cult V,5**
4. Number Five Gully III*
5. Number Six Gully IV,4**
6. Chaos Chimney III*

## Amphitheatre Scoop Direct 240m V,5***

*I.S. Clough, G. Lowe and J. Hardie, February 1966*

One of the best climbs on the face. To the right of the middle tier of D Buttress is a well-defined gully with a steep ice pitch above Middle Ledge; start beneath the lower tier directly below this gully. Climb the lower tier by a steep ice chimney (crux) and continue by the ice pitch to gain the easy upper gully.

## Amphitheatre North Ridge 100m II,3**

*I.S. Clough and party, 27 January 1969*

Starts above and slightly right of the easy upper gully of Amphitheatre Scoop and goes up a series of cracks and grooves in the fine crest.

## Number Four Gully 300m IV,4*

*J. Brown and D. Whillans, December 1952*

The obvious deep gully near the centre of the face has several pitches in the lower part, but unfortunately rarely is its deep-cleft finish in true condition.

## Elliot's Downfall 115m V,6***

*D. Cuthbertson, February 1979*

The gigantic icicle below Number Five Gully gives a steep and serious lead. Two easier pitches then lead to Number Five Gully. It was the downfall of Elliot's proclamation that it would never be climbed that gave the route its name – not the fact that it's prone to collapse when it is climbed! It formed and was climbed in 2021 and in 1996. If you see it formed, make sure you take the opportunity to climb it.

## Number Six Gully 240m IV,4***

*D. Munro and P. Smith, 30 March 1951*

The long gully on the right side of the face usually gives about four good pitches, the last one being the crux. A popular climb and recommended, but the rock below Middle Ledge is very poor for belays, and snow anchors might be necessary. A quick descent can be made by climbing up right via a chimney, 50m after the crux pitch, to a series of ledges, which lead right above steep ground and descend into Coire nam Beitheach opposite Deep-Cut Chimney. There's also a direct finish up another pitch of steeper ice.

## Bidean nam Bian 1150m (NN 143 542)

| | |
|---|---|
| **Start** | Car park at Loch Achtriochtan (NN 139 567) |
| **Time** | 2hr 15min |
| **Crag base altitude** | 950m |
| **Route lengths** | 50–250m |
| **Route styles** | Rocky and turfy mixed climbing |
| **Avalanches** | The approach slopes and descent routes can be quite avalanche prone – the long slope beneath Church Door Buttress in particular. |

The summit cliffs of Bidean nam Bian consist of two main buttresses divided by a gully – Central Gully. The right-hand buttress is called Church Door Buttress, the left-hand one Diamond Buttress. Collie's Pinnacle is the square buttress at the foot of Central Gully, dividing the gully in two.

### Approach
Walk past the cottage at Achnambeithach on the outside of the fence and follow the fence to the stream coming out of Number Two Gully. Cross the stream and continue to follow bits of fence posts up underneath the west face of Aonach Dubh to some prominent boulders at the entrance to Coire nam Beitheach. By following the old fence line all the way up, you'll get to some prominent boulders at the entrance to Coire nam Beitheach. Follow the north-east side of the stream to reach Diamond Buttress, Church Door Buttress or Bishop's Buttress, with a last steep slope that can be quite avalanche prone.

An alternative approach starts through a gate immediately west of the road bridge spanning the River Coe. The path climbs steeply to the south (beware of an icy patch on the path) and after about 1hr levels off into a short gorge. At this point it's better to descend to the stream bed and follow either side of the stream in the gorge. Access to the west face of Aonach Dubh can be made from here and, from the top of the gorge, to Church Door Buttress and Stob Coire nam Beith.

# Diamond Buttress and Church Door Buttress

Church Door Buttress

Diamond Buttress

Crypt Route IV,6***

Collie's Pinnacle

① North Route III*
①a North Route – Direct Start III
② Diamond Route V,6*
③ Direct Route V,6**
④ Koh-i-nor V,7*
⑤ Fever Pitch V,7
⑥ Central Gully I***
⑦ Knights Templar VII,8*
⑧ West Chimney Route V,6**

> **Descent**
> From Diamond Buttress, go north-east to the col before Stob Coire nan Lochan and descend back into the corrie. From Church Door Buttress and Bishop's Buttress, descend the small corrie north between the two tops of Bidean nam Bian back to the foot of either buttress. Retreat can be made from Church Door Buttress by an exciting 60m abseil from the arch into Central Gully.
>
> A subsidiary corrie leads up between the cliffs of Bishop's Buttress and Stob Coire nam Beith to a shallow col between the two summits; this gives another descent route.

## DIAMOND BUTTRESS

### North Route 210m III*
*J. Clarkson and F. King, 6 February 1955*
Skirts round the left end of the buttress following a series of chimneys and scoops which lead to a final rocky arête. Easy escapes are possible to the left. A slightly more difficult **direct start** (grade III, *L.S. Lovat and W. Harrison, March 1955*) is to follow an obvious steep scoop near, but to the right of, the normal route which leads to an arête on the right. The arête is followed by a traverse into another scoop, and then the line goes up and left to join the normal route at about 80m.

### Diamond Route 255m V,6*
*D. Rubens and G. Cohen, 9 February 1986*
Start in a bay midway between the toe of the buttress and Collie's Pinnacle. Gain the left-trending ramp and follow it and go further left (40m). Climb steeply to belay below a short V-chimney (30m). Avoid the chimney awkwardly to the right and go straight up, continuing to the upper girdle ledge (65m). Go right to the end of the ledge (60m). Climb a short difficult chimney to an arête and then to the top (60m).

### Direct Route 150m V,6**
*M. Noon and J. MacLean, January 1959*
Find a way up the central wall of the buttress to gain the right end of a long ledge which cuts across the face. Continue by grooves up and then to the right to emerge on the right-hand ridge shortly below the summit. A solid coating of good snow/ice is essential for this route.

### Central Gully 180m I or II**

*N. Collie, G.A. Sollie and J. Collier, March 1894*

A fine route but with some avalanche risk. Start to the right of Collie's Pinnacle and continue directly to the top up easy slopes. By taking a start to the left of the pinnacle and using the right fork near the top, a good climb of grade II standard will be found.

## CHURCH DOOR BUTTRESS

To the right of Collie's Pinnacle at the foot of Central Gully, a wide spur divides Church Door buttress into two facets. The east face overlooks Central Gully and west face towers above the easy but steep snow slopes ascending towards the summit of Bidean.

### Un Poco Loco Direct Direct 120m VII,7**

*A. Cave and M. Duff, March 1994 (original route); E. Tresidder and I. Lewis, 14 February 2005 (Direct Finish)*

Climb a series of cracked corners left of Crypt Route, past a worrying block at 12m (20m). Climb up towards The Arch by a shallow right-facing corner and up through the hole at the back to a belay in the middle of the span (35m). Go directly above the left end of the span to a groove and flake-crack, then trend gradually left (25m). Easier to the top (40m).

### Crypt Route 60m IV,6***

*H. MacInnes and party, February 1960*

An unusual route winding its way through passages in the right wall of Central Gully. A bit more like caving than climbing, but none the worse for it. Climb the first pitch of Central Gully and move right to climb a steep chimney in the buttress. Where it closes, step left and move into the Crypt, generally trying to move upwards to find a chamber and a very tight squeeze to emerge at The Arch, a platform above the initial chimney. Move around onto the top of The Arch and finish as for West Chimney Route. Not a route for larger people. Take a torch and leave your rucksack at the bottom!

### Flake Route, Right Hand 190m V,7**

*R. Anderson and R. Milne, 26 February 2005*

Starting at the entrance of the right-hand start of Central Gully, this route climbs the right-hand side of the huge flake. Just below the chockstone in the gully, climb a series of corners on the right to ledges and continue to belay at the fork in the

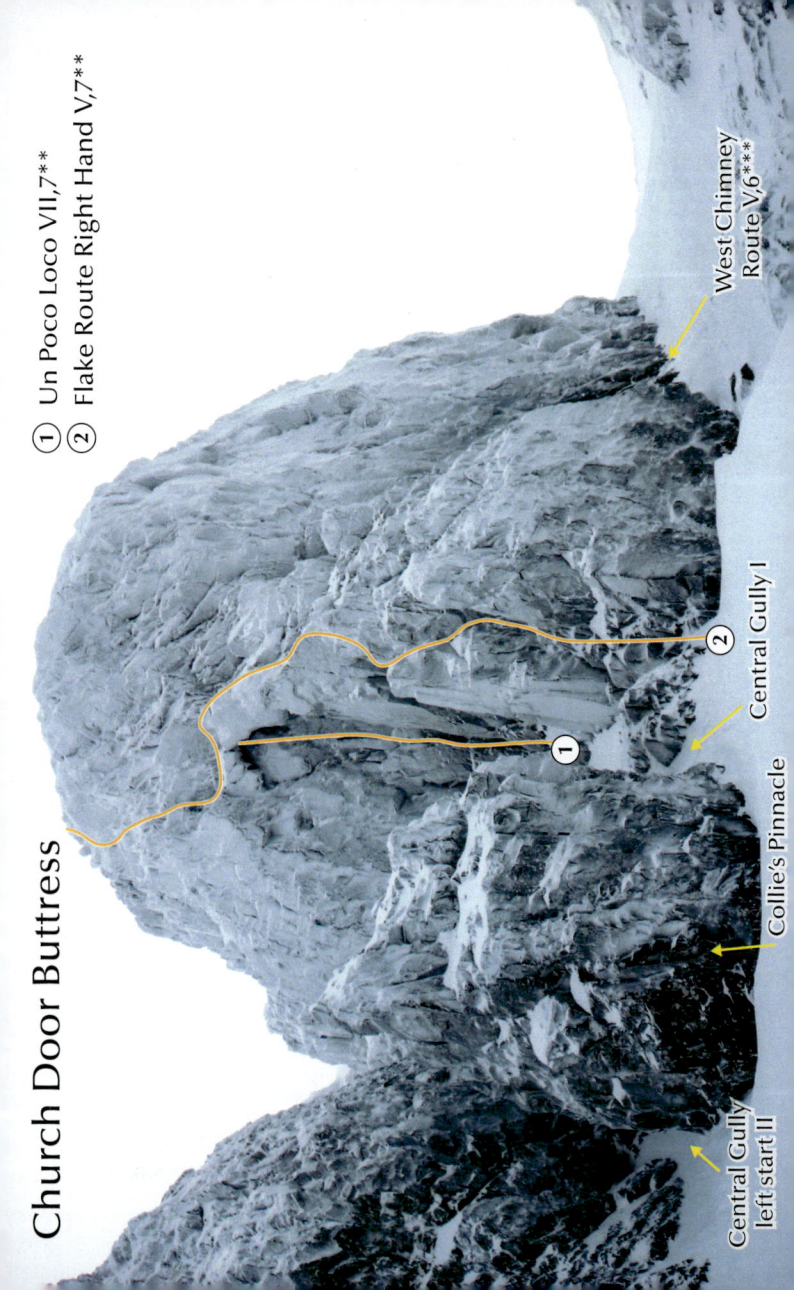

*Deep in Crypt Route*

chimney above (40m). Follow the widening left fork over chockstones then tunnel under the huge jammed blocks to belay at the col at the top of the flake (25m). Go up and right awkwardly then straight up broken ground until it's possible to traverse left to The Arch. Cross The Arch and climb a shallow chimney (crux) followed by grooves and walls to the top.

### Knights Templar 150m VII,8**
*I. Small and B. Fyffe, January 2007*
A fine direct line following the crest of the buttress and cutting across West Chimney. Start just to the left of the toe of the buttress. Climb a wide crack and the wall to the left to a terrace (20m). Climb the obvious groove to a steep exit then easier ground to a hole/cave where Flake Route comes in (40m). Continue up moderate ground to belay by the boulder on West Chimney Route above The Arch (50m). Climb a steep groove in the arête just behind the boulder to a shelf. Climb up a groove at the left of the shelf, step right at a spike to another groove and follow this to a chimney-groove. Climb this to easier ground (40m).

### West Chimney Route 180m V,6***
*A. Fyffe and H. MacInnes, 8 February 1969*
Up to the right of the lowest rocks of the buttress is a snowy bay leading to an obvious deep chimney, which is followed past two difficult chockstones to a bay. A very steep short wall above leads to a ledge. The wide chimney above narrows and ends on a shelf which is traversed left around a corner to the top of The Arch, an airy platform formed by two huge jammed boulders. From the left end of The Arch, climb a 10m corner chimney and flake-crack, then trend gradually left (25m). Easier to the top (40m).

## WEST TOP OF BIDEAN NAM BIAN

Slightly higher up the corrie, these cliffs are on the western flank of the spur that descends northwards into Coire nam Beitheach from the West Top of Bidean nam Bian. The lower end of this ridge ends at Bishop's Buttress (NN 142 544).

(photo: Donald King)

# Bidean nam Bian

1. West Chimney Route V,6***
2. The Gangway II
3. The Fang V,6
4. Closer IV,5**
5. St Peter's Well VI,7**
6. Return of the Nedi VI,5**
7. Parthian Shot V,7
8. The Gash IV, 4**
9. The Hash III
10. Hourlass Gully I
11. Dubiety IV,5*
12. Minute Man IV,5*

### The Crook 50m VI,7

*D. King and A. Nelson, 28 December 2003*
(no photo topo)
The prominent crack line up the centre of the north face of Bishop's Buttress. Climb the crack to a right-sloping ledge and follow this into a bay. Climb a left-slanting groove and short wall to reach another bay with a rocking block (35m). Climb the corner above and exit left (15m).

### Closer 75m IV,5**
*C. Dale, A. Kassyk and D. Talbot, 18 February 1982*
Starts some distance below The Gash beyond broken ground. A prominent steep chimney with an icefall beneath it. Climb the icefall, chimney, bulges and chockstones to the top.

### St Peter's Well 50m VI,7**
*B. Davison, S. Kennedy and D. Wilkinson, 13 January 2001*
The left of three corner lines approached by a short steep groove on the left. Two hard sections in the corner lead to icy grooves.

### Return of the Nedi 90m IV,5**
*S. Kennedy and A. Nelson, 29 December 2000*
The central corner line gives good sustained climbing.

### The Gash 120m IV,4**
*I. Clough, M. Hadley and M. Large, 22 March 1959*
The steep cliffs below Hourglass Gully are split by a narrow, deep-cleft gully gained by a rising traverse leftwards from Hourglass Gully, or it may be reached directly. This gives a series of short bulging pitches barred at the top by a chockstone. Climb this on the left to a cave below a second huge chockstone. An intriguing through-route should be possible.

### Hourglass Gully 120m I
*I. Clough and party, February 1966*
The long tapering gully right of The Gash which opens into a snow fan near the top. Steep but straightforward.

---

*Stob Coire nam Beith 1107m (NN 139 545)*

---

| | |
|---|---|
| **Start** | Car park at Loch Achtriochtan (NN 139 567) |
| **Time** | 1hr 45min |
| **Crag base altitude** | 750m |
| **Route lengths** | 90–500m |
| **Route styles** | Cascade ice, mixed rock and ice |
| **Avalanches** | Take care in the big gullies and on the descent slopes. |

The climbing on this mountain offers length, quality and variety. It will test the ability to find a route without a detailed description, especially higher up the climbs, where many different options will be found. It's a fine peak for middle-grade mountaineering routes.

The base of this massive and complicated cone of cliffs swings through a great arc, so that not all the climbs can be seen from the junction of the stream on the approach route. The most obvious feature here is the long Summit Gully. The slabby 90m Pyramid and (above and left of it) the bigger and steeper Sphinx Buttress form an indefinite ridge which bounds Summit Gully on the left. To the left of these is the region where the vague North-West Gully winds its way through the broken rocks of Number Four Buttress. The central section contains the rightward-slanting ramp gully start of North-West Gully, Deep-Cut Chimney and the long shallow ice course of Central Gully.

Beyond Central Gully, the cliffs on the left-hand side of the cone fall back and eventually form a very big bay. Arch Gully runs up the right-hand side of the bay, and to the left of the lower part of this is a big rock rognon split by a narrow chimney line, the start of the so-called Number One Buttress. Above this rognon is a broad sloping snow shelf and the continuation of the Number One Buttress chimney-line, which leads up the rocks at the back of the bay.

A shallow gully curls up and round the left-hand side of the rognon to the snow shelf. This is the approach to Broken Gully, which has two forks and lies in the left-hand recess of the bay. It leads up to the left to emerge on a shoulder. Beyond Broken Gully, the final bold projection below the shoulder is called Zero Buttress.

## Approach

Walk along the A82 over the road bridge spanning the River Coe. Go through a gate immediately west of the bridge and find the path leading up the west side of Allt Coire nam Beithach. Follow this path past waterfalls and through the gorge into Coire nam Beitheach.

Three streams depart from a junction at the top of the gorge (NN 139 553). The vague central branch leads up into Summit Gully; this stream approach can provide a good reference point for people climbing on these complicated cliffs. The left-hand stream can also be followed in a south-easterly direction through a steep band of rock bluffs into the corrie beneath

> the cliffs. A waterfall will be encountered on this approach and is best avoided to the right (west).
>
> **Descent**
> From the summit, walk west and descend to Bealach An t-Sròn. Descend back into the corrie from here.

### Zero Buttress 115m IV,4*
*S. Kennedy and R. Hamilton, 26 February 2006*
(no photo topo)
Based on the prominent right-facing corner in the buttress immediately left of The Corridors. Climb directly into the base of the corner, then traverse to slabs right of the corner (25m). Cross the slab diagonally rightwards to a large block on the right edge, overlooking The Corridors. Surmount the block and follow an open groove to a short wall (45m). Climb a steep slab just left of the wall, then mixed ground before moving left on snow to finish by an easy groove (40m).

### The Corridors 160m III/IV,4*
*I. Clough, M.A. Hudson, C. Hutchinson, C. Williamson and D. Davies, 12 February 1969*
(no photo topo)
To the left of Broken Gully, the face of Zero Buttress is cut by two shallow square-cut gully sections: the first ending at a ledge about 45m up, and the other starting from this ledge a little further to the right and leading to the top of the buttress. This gives the line of the climb. The first corridor is often only filled with powder snow, so a better alternative is to take the ice ribbon leading directly up the lower slabs to the second corridor. This should then give a couple of steep pitches leading to easier ground.

### Number One Buttress 270m II/III*
*I. Clough and party, 9 March 1967*
(no photo topo)
The chimney line up the rognon left of Arch Gully and the upper tier above gives a series of short ice pitches leading to the shoulder on Arch Gully.

### Arch Gully 270m III*
*C.M. Allen and J.H.B. Bell, December 1933*
To the left the main area of rocks is Arch Gully. The first section is generally banked up and leads under the arch formed by a chockstone. Above, a couple

# Stob Coire nam Beith

1. Central Gully IV,4**
2. Crack Climb IV,4
3. Deep-Cut Chimney IV,4***
4. North-West Gully III**
   slanting ramp start

Arch Gully III*

North-West Gully III**

of steep pitches are climbed directly to a shoulder. Continue to the summit or traverse off to the left.

### Central Gully 450m IV,4**
*J. Clarkson and J. Waddell, 12 January 1958*
To the left of Crack Climb an ice-trap can form. Climb the ice-trap and follow the gully above via three to four steep pitches to easier ground. A fine climb.

### Deep-Cut Chimney 450m IV,4***
*W.M. MacKenzie and W.H. Murray, April 1939*
The obvious deep narrow gully starting just to the left of the slanting ramp is a classic climb. The lower part gives two or three steep pitches leading at 130m to a small amphitheatre, from where escape right is possible. Go up left from the amphitheatre over iced rocks to a long steep crack-line which leads to easier ground. A further 200m to the summit.

### North-West Gully 500m III**
*Glover and Worsdell, April 1906*
Sometimes mistaken for Summit Gully to its right, but distinguished by its lack of real entry and by a slanting ramp cutting in from the left below Number Four Buttress. Open to considerable variation. The best start is by the slanting ramp, but steep and harder direct entries can be used. Easy snow then leads to a fork. The left branch lacks interest, so go right to another fork amid impressive scenery. From here go to a shoulder from where a steep wall leads to easier ground.

> On the right side of North-West Gully are two buttresses, one above the other. These form a ridge on the left of Summit Gully. The wedge-like lower buttress is The Pyramid and above is The Sphinx. Immediately left of and higher than The Sphinx is the steep column of The Mummy.

### The Sphinx 135m IV,5**
*J.R. Marshall and I. Douglas, 12 January 1958*
(no photo topo)
Climb North-West Gully until below a long black cave about halfway up. Start below and left of this cave by a shattered wall and climb to a small basin below the cave. Go right to a platform under the steep upper rocks. Climb high-stepped walls to reach the obvious chimney above (20m) and gain a tiny recess 3m up to the right. Grasp the top edge of a pinnacle-flake on the right-hand side, swing into space and start climbing for the top (75m); sustained!

### Cleftweave 450m II/III*

*B. Clarke and A. Strachan, January 1972*
(no photo topo)
Well to the right of North-West Gully, follow a series of gullies which wind up left of The Pyramid to overlook Summit Gully. A steep short ice wall on the left is followed to gullies and a snow bowl. Follow a gully and ice pitch on the right to exit on summit slopes.

### The Pyramid 90m III*

*J.R. Marshall and I. Douglas, 12 January 1958*
(no photo topo)
Begin at the lowest rocks above the start of North-West Gully and follow the north ridge to the top.

### Summit Gully 500m II**

(no photo topo)
The great long gully which starts just to the left of the lowest rocks of the Stob Coire nam Beith cone of cliffs. This route is often mistaken for North-West Gully. If snow has obliterated the vague, central stream bed mentioned in the earlier approach description, look for the most obvious and continuous gully line of least resistance descending from just right (west) of the summit. This is well seen from the stream junction of the approach route.

The route is generally straightforward, with a possibility of ice steps to start with. A large cave pitch at mid-height might be impossible but can be turned by a right-hand gully branch 50m lower down. Above the cave it's straightforward to the exit, which is just right of the summit cairn.

## AN T-SRÒN 907M (NN 134 548)

### The Chasm of An t-Sròn 360m IV,4*

*H.M. Brown, J. Matyssek, R.K. Graham and M. Smith, 2 January 1963*
(no photo topo)
The great gully splitting the north face. The first pitch is normally turned, but the other pitches higher up in the right-hand branches give good sport in icy conditions.

# GLEN COE – OUTLYING AREAS

*Captain Hook, Cut-Throat and Peter Pan Direct on Beinn Udlaidh*

## Beinn Udlaidh 840m (NN 280 332)

| | |
|---|---|
| **Start** | Close to Glen Orchy Farm on the B8074 (NN 260 347) |
| **Time** | 1hr |
| **Crag base altitude** | 550–650m |
| **Route lengths** | 75–180m |
| **Route styles** | Cascade ice climbing |
| **Avalanches** | Deceptively large cornices and slopes can line the tops of some of these climbs, and avalanches occur here quite often when the climbs are in condition. |
| **Note** | Parking space at the start is limited and this can be a popular venue. Park as sensitively as possible. |

This low-lying cliff in Coire Daimh, west of the summit, is included in this guide due to its proximity to Glen Coe and its collection of high-quality cascade ice climbs. Being at such a low altitude, a prolonged good, solid frost is required to harden up the springs that flow down the cliff and produce the climbs. A small selection of the more popular routes is described.

Access to the cliff is by driving down Glen Orchy to the entrance of Glen Orchy Farm, where limited roadside parking can be found. This is where Allt Daimh joins the River Orchy. Please park responsibly and avoid walking straight through the farm. The owners are very nice and supportive, but it's important to be discreet and behave responsibly.

### Approach
Avoid the farmhouse by walking on the outside of the fields close to the farm, on the south side. Find the steep track that climbs through the forest into Coire Daimh. Traverse into and cross the floor of the corrie to reach the climbs.

### Descent
Walk left or right to the end of the crags and then down into the corrie basin.

The climbs are described from left to right.

# BEINN UDLAIDH

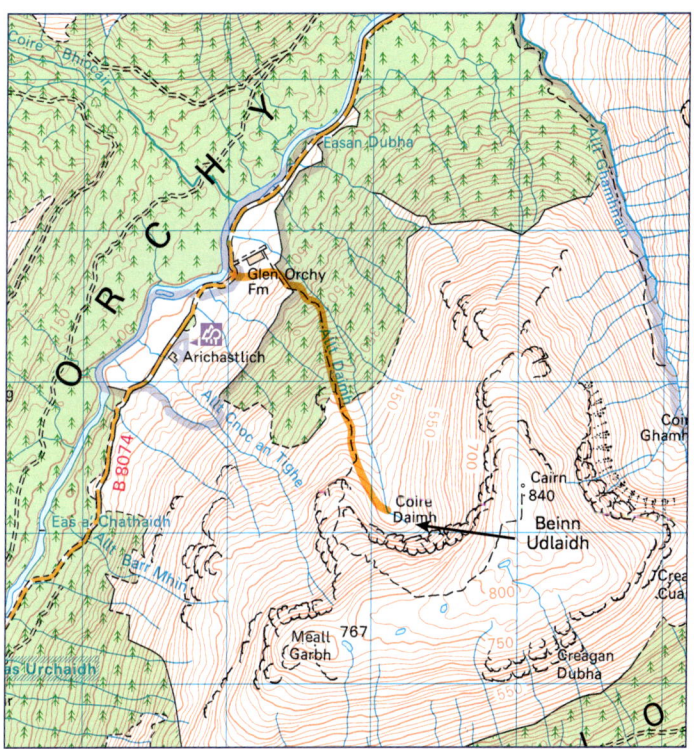

### Quartzvein Scoop 90m IV,4***
*D. Evans, A. Gray and A. Shepherd, 1979*
A steep diagonal line immediately left of the steep Black Wall.

### Captain Hook 75m VI,6***
*D. Cuthbertson and C. Calow, January 1980*
Ascends the funnel-shaped cascade in the centre of the Black Wall.

### Cut-Throat 75m VI,6***
*D. Cuthbertson, R. Duncan, R. Young and C. Calow, January 1980*
The obvious icicle which is often not complete and may require a free pull on occasions.

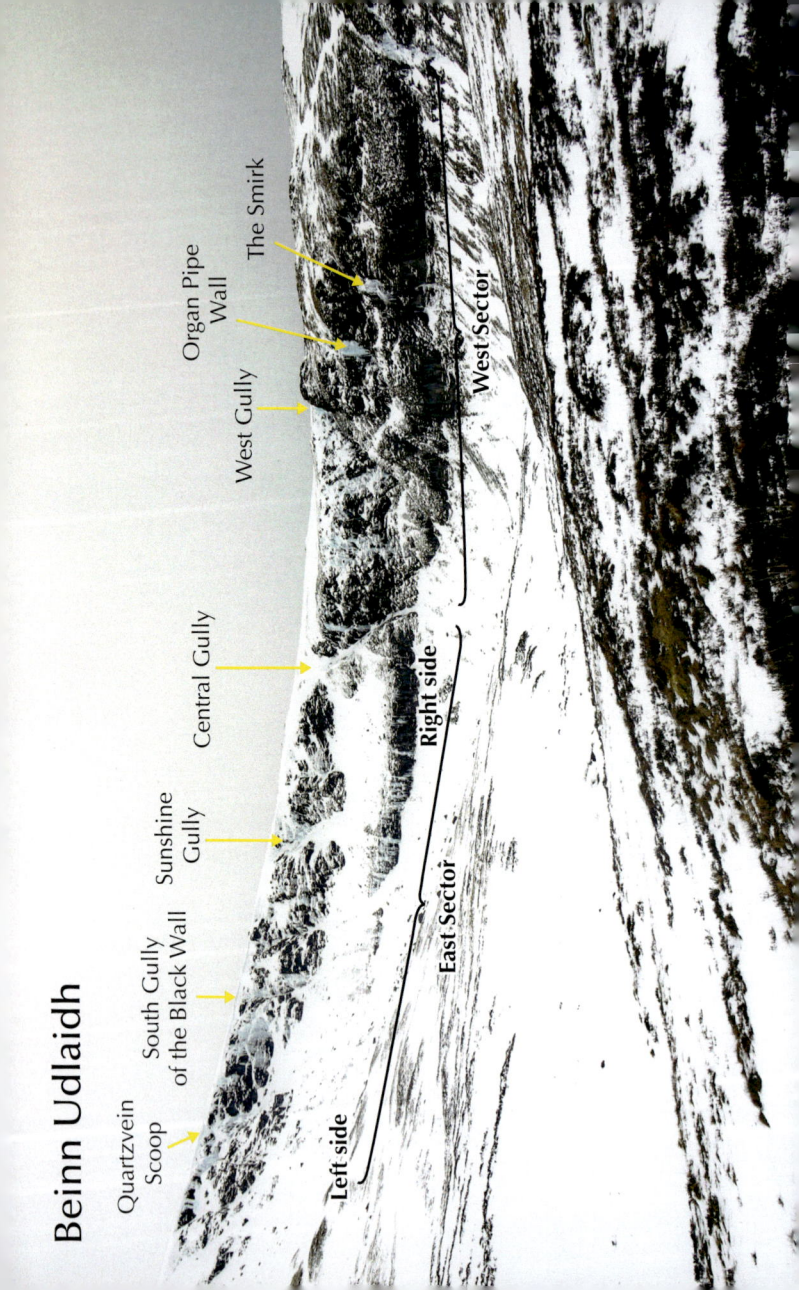

### Peter Pan Direct 85m V,5***
*D. Claxton, I. Duckworth, A. Kay and N. Morrison, 1 January 1982*
Climb the right-hand of two obvious icefalls directly to the top.

### South Gully of Black Wall 120m IV,4***
*R. McGowan and G. Skelton, 30 November 1969*
The first obvious gully to the right of the ice-draped Black Wall.

### Ramshead Gully 120m III*
*G.H. Caplan and I.D. Crofton, 4 December 1976*
To the right of South Gully is a steep rocky buttress; Ramshead Gully is on its right. Exit right at the top.

### Sunshine Gully 90m III,3***
*E. Fowler, F. Jack, R. McGowan and G. Skelton, 14 November 1970*
Midway between South Gully of Black Wall and Central Gully. It appears as a left-trending ramp and can contain plenty of ice.

### Central Gully 180m II
*J. Buchanan, J. Forbes and G. Skelton, 29 December 1968*
The long left-trending gully in the centre of the corrie. In lean conditions it can contain four ice pitches.

### Doctor's Dilemma 180m IV,4**
*I. Duckworth and M. Firth, 1978*
On the buttress to the right of Central Gully. Climbs the prominent wide central series of cascades. Starts up left of the toe of the buttress.

### Junior's Jangle 90m IV,4*
*J.G. Fraser and N. Morrison, 30 December 1979*
Start a little way up West Gully and follow a series of corners to the right of centre of the buttress on the left.

### West Gully 180m III**
The obvious right-trending gully.

The next two routes start from within the hidden deep chimney.

# Beinn Udlaidh East Sector Left Side

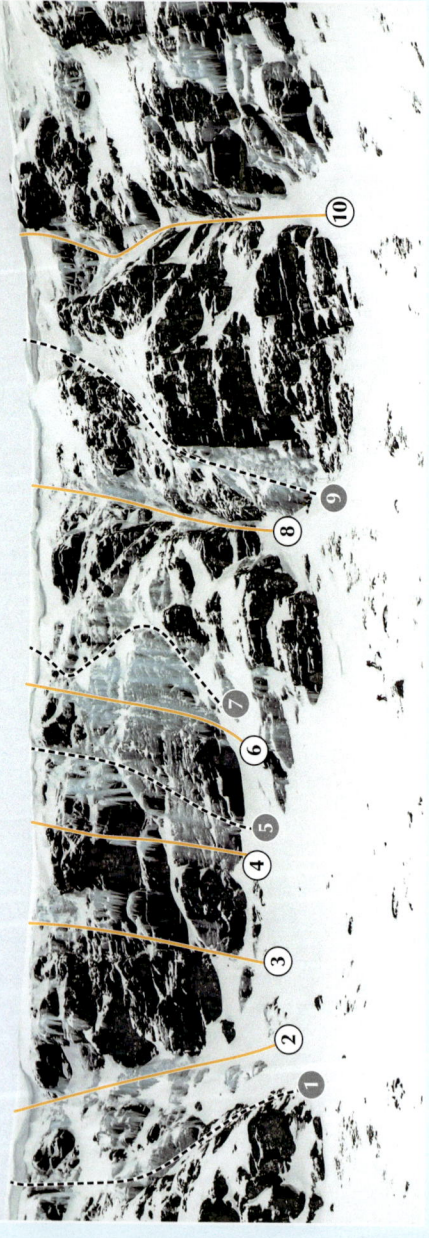

1. Ice Crew III,3**
2. Quartzvein Scoop IV,4***
3. Captain Hook VI,6***
4. Cut-Throat VI,6***
5. The Croc V,5**
6. Peter Pan Direct V,5***
7. Land of Make Believe II**
8. South Gully of Black Wall IV,4***
9. Green Eyes IV,4*
10. Ramshead Gully III*

### Organ Pipe Wall 75m V,5**
R. Duncan and J.G. Fraser, 27 January 1979
Climbs the obvious cascade directly by a central groove and wall.

### The Smirk 90m V,5***
R. Duncan and J.G. Fraser, 27 January 1979
The prominent steep chimney-gully on the right-hand side of the West Wall. Left fork or direct finishes are possible. Slow to come into condition.

## LOCHABER – OTHER AREAS

### SGÙRR NA H-ULAIDH 994M (NN 111 518)

This fine but remote peak lies to the west of Bidean and has several easy climbs on the north face of the mountain. The conspicuous, deep gully directly below the summit gives three or four good pitches of ice climbing and is called Red Gully: 200m, grade III**.

**Note:** This is a difficult mountain to descend from in poor visibility.

### BEINN A' BHEITHIR

These two munros – Sgorr Dhearg, 1024m (NN 056 558) and Sgorr Dhonuill, 1001m (NN 040 555) – are known collectively as the Ballachulish Horseshoe, and stand high above Loch Linnhe looking down to the Sound of Mull.

### The School House Ridge 580m I*
(no photo topo)
This is the north-east ridge of Sgorr Bhan (NN 062 560) above Ballachulish primary school and is an interesting route under snowy conditions. It is quite turfy and requires a good freeze, and has fantastic views up Glen Coe and Loch Leven.

### The Dragon's Tooth 700m II**
(no photo topo)
Above Gleann a Chaolais and the Dragons Tooth golf course is a peak known as the Dragon's Tooth, more appropriately called Sgorr a Chaolais. The ridge going

*Schoolhouse Ridge of Sgorr Dhearg*

south from the top of this tooth to its junction with the ridge leading to the summit of Sgorr Dhonuill gives an interesting scramble with atmosphere.

To gain the ridge, go up the good access path from the top left of the glen (Eastern Coire) to above the forest, and climb a grade II snow gully on the east side (NN 045 562). It's also possible to gain the tooth more steeply from the Western Coire. When going south along the ridge, a vertical downward step will be reached. Turn this on the east side or abseil.

## BEINN FHIONNLAIDH 959M (NN 095 497)

### Rapunzel 350m IV**
(no photo topo)
*S. Richardson and R. Clothier, 11 January 1987*
Access from the south via Glen Creran, off the A828 (NN 035 488). A deep chasm splitting the south face of the mountain. Being at such a low altitude and facing

*Sgorr Dhonuill*

south, a good hard frost is needed to provide decent conditions. A route of great variety, similar to Dalness Chasm in Glen Etive. If Blue Riband is frozen up, this will be good too. Where the gully splits, take the right fork.

## GARBH BHEINN 885M (NM 904 622)

Across on the west side of Loch Linnhe is a wonderful small mountain called Garbh Bheinn – 'the rough mountain'. Made of fabulous grippy gneiss, it's great for rock climbing and scrambling and has recently seen lots of interest by mixed climbers. Several hard snowed-up rock climbs now exist on the South Wall, directly below the summit, often on high-quality established rock climbs. As with all winter climbs, make sure the rocks are white with rime and properly frozen when you climb here.

Any climbing trip that involves a boat is going to be good! Take the ferry at Corran and drive south-west then west to the col at a cattle grid. Park in an

## Winter Climbs: Glen Coe

> old section of road on the left (NM 897 603) and walk up the east side of Allt a' Chothruim. Continue up very steep slopes to the col at 748m (NM 904 619) in about 1hr 30min. To get to The Great Ridge and The Great Gully, descend 170m north-east from here then go north to find the starts of the climbs.

### The Great Ridge 300m IV,4**

A. Matthewson and, J. MacLaurin, 11 January 1987
(no photo topo)
Start at the lowest rocks, about 50 metres left of The Great Gully. The summer route climbs a wet slab into a right-trending ramp. In winter, find a turfy line to the right of the summer line to gain big grassy terraces. Work up and right to the foot of the main ridge. Follow the crest of the rocky ridge as well as you can to the top.

### The Great Gully 300m VI,6**

C. Bonington, T.W. Patey and D. Whillans, 20 February 1969
(no photo topo)
A very strong team of first ascensionists climbed the gully direct, with the Left Fork Finish. The first sections are on cascade ice, with long sections of snow. A deep

Climbing The Great Gully, Garbh Bheinn

cave about halfway up might be climbed on steep cascade ice on the left side, or avoided on the right starting 40m lower down the gully. Above more easy snow, the Left Fork Finish is an obvious slot providing mixed climbing with a steep pull at the top.

## STOB A' GHLAIS CHOIRE 996M (NN 240 516)

Well seen from the Kingshouse, the north-east face of this mountain appears to be seamed with steep gullies and ridges. On closer inspection the angle relents. However, this area is worthwhile for climbers looking for easier ascents away from the crowds.

Access is governed by the amount of water in the River Etive. When the river's low it's possible to cross at a number of spots, either before or after Coupall Bridge (NN 243 543), and skirt the foot of Creag Dhubh. Allow 1hr 30min for either approach.

In descent, the corrie south-east of the summit of Stob a' Ghlais Choire can be taken. Care should be exercised on these slopes after strong winds or snowfalls, as wind-slab avalanches may be present. A longer but more satisfying end to a climb would involve ascending both Creise (1110m) and Meall a' Bhùiridh (1108m). A descent could then be made through the ski area to the north.

### Inglis Clark Ridge 140m III*
*R. Napier and S. Downie, March 1987*
(no photo topo)
In the centre of the north-east face is a broad V-shaped buttress just left of a fairly obvious gully, the top of which is a flat-topped tower. Start at the right-hand end of the ridge, 30m up the gully. Follow grooves and some steep ice pitches (crux) to a broad terrace (35m). Ascend to the rock tower and climb it on the right to a wall (65m). Traverse left (5m) along the wall and then up right by blocks and a right-angled corner chimney to the top of the tower.

# APPENDIX A
## Useful contacts

**Weather**

Mountain Weather Information Service
www.mwis.org.uk/forecasts/scottish/west-highlands

Met Office
www.metoffice.gov.uk/weather/specialist-forecasts/mountain/southwest-highlands

Weather data from Aonach Mòr at 1200m
https://holfuy.com/en/weather/1365

Weather data from Aonach Mòr at 900m
https://holfuy.com/en/weather/195

Weather data from Aonach Mòr at 650m
https://holfuy.com/en/weather/296

Webcam images and weather data from CIC Hut, Ben Nevis
www.smc.org.uk/cicwebcam/cic_weather.php

Glencoe Mountain weather data
www.glencoemountain.co.uk/weather

**Avalanche forecasts and safety**

Scottish Avalanche Information Service (SAIS)
www.sais.gov.uk

Be Avalanche Aware (BAA) guidance
http://beaware.sais.gov.uk

**Emergencies**

Mountain rescue tel 999 (ask for police, then ask for mountain rescue)

emergencySMS
www.emergencysms.net

**Scottish mountaineering resources**

Scottish Mountaineering Club (SMC)
www.smc.org.uk

Mountaineering Scotland
www.mountaineering.scot

Scottish Outdoor Access Code
www.nature.scot

**Accommodation**

Fort William and Glencoe accommodation
www.outdoorcapital.co.uk/stay

Fort William guesthouses
http://fortwilliam-guesthouse.com

Mountaineering Scotland/BMC huts
www.mountaineering.scot/clubs/huts/national-huts

CIC hut, Ben Nevis
www.smc.org.uk/huts/cic

**Transport**

**Bike hire in Fort William**
Nevis Cycles
www.neviscycles.com

Off Beat Bikes
www.offbeatbikes.co.uk

**Car hire in Fort William**
EasyDrive
www.easydrivescotland.co.uk

Practical Car & Van Rental
www.practical.co.uk/locations/england/scotland/fortwilliam

# APPENDIX B
*Route summary table by area*

## Appendix B – Route summary table by area

This is the order in which the routes appear in this guide.

| Route name | Area | Route length (metres) | Overall grade | Technical grade | Main style | Sub-style(s) | Rating | Page |
|---|---|---|---|---|---|---|---|---|
| **Aonach Eagach** | | | | | | | | 51 |
| Aonach Eagach Traverse | Aonach Eagach | 3000 | III | - | Mixed | Rock | *** | 53 |
| Blue Riband | Aonach Eagach | 600 | V | 5 | Ice | Cascade | *** | 54 |
| Vice Chancellor Ridge | Aonach Eagach | 210 | III | - | Mixed | Turf | ** | 54 |
| The Chancellor | Aonach Eagach | 400 | IV | - | Mixed | Turf | ** | 54 |
| Chancellor Gully | Aonach Eagach | 500 | III/IV | - | Ice | Cascade | ** | 55 |
| Bodach Buttress | Aonach Eagach | 120 | III | 4 | Mixed | Turf | * | 55 |
| **Buachaille Etive Mòr** | | | | | | | | 55 |
| The Chasm | Stob Dearg | 450 | V | 6 | Ice | Cascade | *** | 58 |
| The Chasm to Crowberry Traverse | Stob Dearg | 1000 | II | - | Snow, mixed | General | * | 60 |
| Lady's Gully | Stob Dearg | 240 | IV | 4 | Ice | Cascade | ** | 60 |
| Direct Route | Stob Dearg | 95 | IV | - | Mixed | General | * | 60 |
| Kinloss Corner | Stob Dearg | 120 | V | 6 | Mixed | General | ** | 61 |
| North Face Route | Stob Dearg | 220 | V | 6 | Mixed | Rock | ** | 61 |

## Winter Climbs: Glen Coe

| Route name | Area | Route length (metres) | Overall grade | Technical grade | Main style | Sub-style(s) | Rating | Page |
|---|---|---|---|---|---|---|---|---|
| Alpen | Stob Dearg | 245 | V | 5 | Mixed | Turf | * | 61 |
| D Gully Buttress | Stob Dearg | 150 | IV | 4 | Mixed | Rock | ** | 62 |
| Curved Ridge | Stob Dearg | 300 | III | 3 | Mixed | Rock | *** | 63 |
| Route I | Stob Dearg | 70 | V | 6 | Mixed | Turf | * | 63 |
| Agag's Groove | Stob Dearg | 105 | VII | 7 | Mixed | Rock | *** | 65 |
| Naismith's Route | Stob Dearg | 200 | IV | 5 | Mixed | Rock | * | 65 |
| Shelf Route | Stob Dearg | 200 | IV | 6 | Mixed | General | ** | 65 |
| Crowberry Gully | Stob Dearg | 300 | IV | 4 | Ice | Snow-ice | *** | 65 |
| North East Zig-Zag | Stob Dearg | 100 | III | - | Ice | Snow-ice | * | 66 |
| North Buttress | Stob Dearg | 300 | IV | 4 | Mixed | Rock or ice | *** | 66 |
| Raven's Gully | Stob Dearg | 135 | V | 6 | Mixed | General | *** | 66 |
| Raven's Edge | Stob Dearg | 170 | VII | 7 | Mixed | General | *** | 67 |
| Cuneiform Buttress, Ordinary Route | Stob Dearg | 135 | IV | 5 | Mixed | General | | 67 |
| The Long Chimney | Stob Dearg | 135 | IV | - | Mixed | General | ** | 68 |
| Great Gully | Stob Dearg | 360 | II/III | - | Ice | Cascade | | 68 |
| Ephemeron Gully | Stob Dearg | 340 | IV | 4 | Ice | Snow-ice | * | 68 |
| Lagangarbh Chimney | Stob Dearg | 60 | III | 4 | Mixed | General | ** | 68 |

## Appendix B – Route summary table by area

| Route name | Area | Route length (metres) | Overall grade | Technical grade | Main style | Sub-style(s) | Rating | Page |
|---|---|---|---|---|---|---|---|---|
| Central Couloir | Stob Coire Altruim | 100 | III | - | Ice | Snow-ice | | 70 |
| Dalmation Couloir | Stob Coire Altruim | 100 | IV | - | Mixed | Turf | *** | 70 |
| **Lairig Eilde** | | | | | | | | 71 |
| Sròn na Lairig | Sròn na Lairig and Eilde Canyon | 300 | II | - | Mixed | Turf | ** | 71 |
| Eilde Canyon | Sròn na Lairig and Eilde Canyon | 30–40 | IV/V | - | Ice | Cascade | | 73 |
| The Bubble | Sròn na Lairig and Eilde Canyon | 60 | III/IV | 4 | Ice | Cascade | *** | 73 |
| **The Lost Valley (Coire Gabhail)** | | | | | | | | 74 |
| Chimney Route | Lost Valley Buttresses | 75 | III/IV | 4 | Mixed | General | * | 78 |
| Right Edge | Lost Valley Buttresses | 120 | IV | 4 | Mixed | Ice | ** | 78 |
| Minor Adjustment | Lost Valley Buttresses | 115 | IV | 5 | Mixed | General | * | 78 |

## WINTER CLIMBS: GLEN COE

| Route name | Area | Route length (metres) | Overall grade | Technical grade | Main style | Sub-style(s) | Rating | Page |
|---|---|---|---|---|---|---|---|---|
| Sabre Tooth | Lost Valley Buttresses | 135 | IV | 5 | Mixed | General | * | 78 |
| Directosaur | Lost Valley Buttresses | 160 | VI | 7 | Mixed | General | * | 80 |
| Pterodactyl (Moonlight Gully) | Lost Valley Buttresses | 110 | V | 6/7 | Mixed | Rock, ice | * | 80 |
| Moonlighting | Lost Valley Buttresses | 120 | V | 6 | Mixed | Rock, turf | * | 81 |
| Neanderthal | Lost Valley Buttresses | 125 | VII | 7 | Mixed | General | *** | 81 |
| Barracuda | Lost Valley Buttresses | 80 | V | 7 | Mixed | General | ** | 81 |
| Gully C | East face of Gearr Aonach | 230 | I | - | Snow | - | | 83 |
| Gully B | East face of Gearr Aonach | 230 | II | - | Mixed | Ice | | 83 |
| Gully A | East face of Gearr Aonach | 235 | IV | 4 | Mixed | Ice | * | 83 |
| Lost Leeper Gully | East face of Gearr Aonach | 300 | III | 4 | Mixed | Ice | ** | 85 |
| Rainmaker | East face of Gearr Aonach | 100 | VI | 5 | Mixed | Ice, rock | ** | 85 |

## Appendix B – Route summary table by area

| Route name | Area | Route length (metres) | Overall grade | Technical grade | Main style | Sub-style(s) | Rating | Page |
|---|---|---|---|---|---|---|---|---|
| Outgrabe Route | East face of Gearr Aonach | 115 | V | 5 | Mixed | Turf, ice | ** | 85 |
| Mome Rath Face Route | East face of Gearr Aonach | 135 | V | 5 | Mixed | Ice, rock | *** | 85 |
| The Wabe | East face of Gearr Aonach | 135 | V | 5 | Ice | Snow patch cascade | *** | 85 |
| Rev Ted's Gully | East face of Gearr Aonach | 300 | III | - | Mixed | Ice | * | 86 |
| Ingrid's Folly and Peregrine Gully | East face of Gearr Aonach | 300 | III | - | Mixed | General | * | 86 |
| The Zig-Zags | East face of Gearr Aonach | 200 | II | - | Mixed | Rock | ** | 88 |
| **Coire nan Lochan** | | | | | | | | |
| Avalanche Gully | North-west face of Gearr Aonach | 300 | IV | 4 | Ice | Cascade | * | 89 |
| Rescue Team Gully | North-west face of Gearr Aonach | 85 | II/III | - | Mixed | Ice | * | 91 |
| 999 | North-west face of Gearr Aonach | 135 | IV | 5 | Mixed | Turf | ** | 91 |

## *Winter Climbs: Glen Coe*

| Route name | Area | Route length (metres) | Overall grade | Technical grade | Main style | Sub-style(s) | Rating | Page |
|---|---|---|---|---|---|---|---|---|
| Boomerang Gully | Stob Coire nan Lochan | 210 | II | - | Snow | - | * | 95 |
| Ordinary Route | Stob Coire nan Lochan | 130 | IV | 5 | Mixed | Turf | ** | 95 |
| The Dual | Stob Coire nan Lochan | 133 | IX | 9 | Mixed | Rock | *** | 96 |
| Scabbard Chimney | Stob Coire nan Lochan | 120 | V | 6 | Mixed | Ice or rock | *** | 96 |
| Spectre | Stob Coire nan Lochan | 120 | V | 6 | Mixed | Ice or rock | ** | 97 |
| Innuendo | Stob Coire nan Lochan | 150 | V | 6 | Mixed | Ice, rock | ** | 97 |
| Langsam | Stob Coire nan Lochan | 200 | II/III | - | Ice | Snow-ice | *** | 97 |
| Broad Gully | Stob Coire nan Lochan | 150 | I | - | Snow | - | * | 97 |
| Dorsal Arête | Stob Coire nan Lochan | 120 | II | 3 | Mixed | Rock | *** | 97 |
| Forked Gully | Stob Coire nan Lochan | 135 | I/II | - | Snow | - | * | 98 |
| Twisting Grooves | Stob Coire nan Lochan | 130 | IV | 5 | Mixed | Turf | ** | 98 |

## Appendix B – Route summary table by area

| Route name | Area | Route length (metres) | Overall grade | Technical grade | Main style | Sub-style(s) | Rating | Page |
|---|---|---|---|---|---|---|---|---|
| Twisting Gully | Stob Coire nan Lochan | 150 | III | 4 | Ice | Snow-ice | ** | 98 |
| Moonshadow | Stob Coire nan Lochan | 150 | IV | 5 | Mixed | Turf | ** | 100 |
| Chimney Route | Stob Coire nan Lochan | 125 | VI | 6 | Mixed | Ice, turf, rock | *** | 100 |
| Tilt | Stob Coire nan Lochan | 140 | VI | 7 | Mixed | Turf | *** | 100 |
| Unicorn | Stob Coire nan Lochan | 125 | VIII | 8 | Mixed | Rock | *** | 100 |
| SC Gully | Stob Coire nan Lochan | 150 | III | 3 | Ice | Snow-ice | *** | 101 |
| East Face Route | Stob Coire nan Lochan | 130 | VI | 7 | Mixed | General | ** | 101 |
| Central Grooves | Stob Coire nan Lochan | 120 | VII | 7 | Mixed | Rock | *** | 101 |
| Central Buttress | Stob Coire nan Lochan | 135 | VII | 7 | Mixed | Rock | *** | 101 |
| Raeburn's Route | Stob Coire nan Lochan | 150 | IV | 4 | Mixed | Turf, ice | *** | 103 |
| NC Gully | Stob Coire nan Lochan | 155 | II | - | Snow | - | ** | 103 |

## Winter Climbs: Glen Coe

| Route name | Area | Route length (metres) | Overall grade | Technical grade | Main style | Sub-style(s) | Rating | Page |
|---|---|---|---|---|---|---|---|---|
| Evening Citizen | Stob Coire nan Lochan | 95 | V | 7 | Mixed | Rock | ** | 103 |
| Para Andy | Stob Coire nan Lochan | 90 | VI | 7 | Mixed | Rock | ** | 103 |
| Intruder | Stob Coire nan Lochan | 100 | V | 7 | Mixed | Rock | ** | 104 |
| Crest Route | Stob Coire nan Lochan | 115 | V | 6 | Mixed | Rock | *** | 104 |
| North Gully | Stob Coire nan Lochan | 75 | I/II | - | Snow | - | | 105 |
| Pinnacle Buttress Groove | Stob Coire nan Lochan | 60 | III | - | Mixed | Ice | * | 105 |
| Orient Express | Far Eastern Buttress | 85 | IV | 5 | Mixed | Turf | * | 106 |
| Eastern Slant | Far Eastern Buttress | 120 | III | 4 | Mixed | Turf | * | 106 |
| Nirvana Wall | Far Eastern Buttress | 75 | VI | 8 | Mixed | Rock | ** | 108 |
| Yen | Far Eastern Buttress | 100 | VI | 7 | Mixed | Rock | | 108 |
| Excellerator | Far Eastern Buttress | 25 | V | 5 | Ice | Snow patch cascade | * | 108 |

## Appendix B – Route summary table by area

| Route name | Area | Route length (metres) | Overall grade | Technical grade | Main style | Sub-style(s) | Rating | Page |
|---|---|---|---|---|---|---|---|---|
| Jane's Weep | Far Eastern Buttress | 25 | VIII | 8 | Ice | Snow patch cascade | * | 108 |
| Darwin's Dihedral | North face of Aonach Dubh | 240 | VI | 6 | Mixed | Ice | ** | 111 |
| Venom | North face of Aonach Dubh | 240 | IV/V | 5 | Mixed | Ice | * | 111 |
| White Snake | North face of Aonach Dubh | 240 | IV | 4 | Mixed | Ice | ** | 111 |
| Findlay's Rise | North face of Aonach Dubh | 240 | IV | 5 | Ice | Cascade | * | 111 |
| Ossian's Close | North face of Aonach Dubh | 240 | III | - | Mixed | Ice | * | 111 |
| Midnight Special | North face of Aonach Dubh | 300 | V | 5 | Mixed | Ice | * | 111 |
| Midnight Cowboy | North face of Aonach Dubh | 370 | V | 6 | Mixed | Ice | ** | 112 |
| Against All Odds | North face of Aonach Dubh | 150 | VI/VII | 7 | Mixed | Ice, turf | ** | 113 |
| Fingal's Chimney | North face of Aonach Dubh | 190 | VI | 7 | Mixed | General | *** | 113 |
| Fall-Out | North face of Aonach Dubh | 125 | VII | 7 | Mixed | General | *** | 113 |

# Winter Climbs: Glen Coe

| Route name | Area | Route length (metres) | Overall grade | Technical grade | Main style | Sub-style(s) | Rating | Page |
|---|---|---|---|---|---|---|---|---|
| **Coire nam Beitheach** | | | | | | | | 114 |
| Dinner-Time Buttress | West face of Aonach Dubh | 335 | II | - | Mixed | Rock | ** | 116 |
| Middle Ledge | West face of Aonach Dubh | 600 | II | - | Mixed | Ice, turf | | 117 |
| Cyclops | West face of Aonach Dubh | 105 | IV | 5 | Mixed | Turf | * | 117 |
| The Pinnacle Face | West face of Aonach Dubh | 110 | IV | 5 | Mixed | Rock | * | 119 |
| Number Three Gully | West face of Aonach Dubh | 300 | III | - | Ice | Snow-ice | *** | 119 |
| The Screen | West face of Aonach Dubh | 75 | IV | 5 | Ice | Snow patch cascade | * | 119 |
| C-D Scoop | West face of Aonach Dubh | 150 | II | - | Ice | Snow-ice | ** | 119 |
| Amphitheatre Scoop Direct | West face of Aonach Dubh | 240 | V | 5 | Mixed | Ice | *** | 121 |
| Amphitheatre North Ridge | West face of Aonach Dubh | 100 | II | 3 | Mixed | Rock | ** | 121 |
| Number Four Gully | West face of Aonach Dubh | 300 | IV | 4 | Mixed | Ice | * | 121 |

## Appendix B – Route summary table by area

| Route name | Area | Route length (metres) | Overall grade | Technical grade | Main style | Sub-style(s) | Rating | Page |
|---|---|---|---|---|---|---|---|---|
| Elliot's Downfall | West face of Aonach Dubh | 115 | V | 6 | Ice | Cascade | *** | 121 |
| Number Six Gully | West face of Aonach Dubh | 240 | IV | 4 | Ice | Snow-ice | *** | 121 |
| North Route | Bidean nam Bian | 210 | III | - | Mixed | Ice | * | 124 |
| Diamond Route | Bidean nam Bian | 255 | V | 6 | Mixed | Ice | * | 124 |
| Direct Route | Bidean nam Bian | 150 | V | 6 | Mixed | Ice | ** | 124 |
| Central Gully | Bidean nam Bian | 180 | I or II | - | Snow | - | ** | 125 |
| Un Poco Loco Direct Direct | Bidean nam Bian | 120 | VII | 7 | Mixed | Rock | ** | 125 |
| Crypt Route | Bidean nam Bian | 60 | IV | 6 | Mixed | Rock | *** | 125 |
| Flake Route, Right Hand | Bidean nam Bian | 190 | V | 7 | Mixed | Rock | ** | 125 |
| Knights Templar | Bidean nam Bian | 150 | VII | 8 | Mixed | Rock | ** | 127 |
| West Chimney Route | Bidean nam Bian | 180 | V | 6 | Mixed | Turf, ice | *** | 127 |

## WINTER CLIMBS: GLEN COE

| Route name | Area | Route length (metres) | Overall grade | Technical grade | Main style | Sub-style(s) | Rating | Page |
|---|---|---|---|---|---|---|---|---|
| The Crook | Bidean nam Bian | 50 | VI | 7 | Mixed | General | | 128 |
| Closer | Bidean nam Bian | 75 | IV | 5 | Mixed | Ice | ** | 129 |
| St Peter's Well | Bidean nam Bian | 50 | VI | 7 | Mixed | Ice | ** | 129 |
| Return of the Nedi | Bidean nam Bian | 90 | IV | 5 | Mixed | General | ** | 129 |
| The Gash | Bidean nam Bian | 120 | IV | 4 | Mixed | General | ** | 129 |
| Hourglass Gully | Bidean nam Bian | 120 | I | - | Snow | - | | 129 |
| Zero Buttress | Stob Coire nam Beith | 115 | IV | 4 | Mixed | General | * | 131 |
| The Corridors | Stob Coire nam Beith | 160 | III/IV | 4 | Ice | Cascade | * | 131 |
| Number One Buttress | Stob Coire nam Beith | 270 | II/III | - | Mixed | Ice | * | 131 |
| Arch Gully | Stob Coire nam Beith | 270 | III | - | Mixed | Ice | * | 131 |
| Central Gully | Stob Coire nam Beith | 450 | IV | 4 | Ice | Cascade | ** | 133 |

## Appendix B – Route summary table by area

| Route name | Area | Route length (metres) | Overall grade | Technical grade | Main style | Sub-style(s) | Rating | Page |
|---|---|---|---|---|---|---|---|---|
| Deep-Cut Chimney | Stob Coire nam Beith | 450 | IV | 4 | Mixed | Ice | *** | 133 |
| North-West Gully | Stob Coire nam Beith | 500 | III | - | Ice | Snow-ice | ** | 133 |
| The Sphinx | Stob Coire nam Beith | 135 | IV | 5 | Mixed | General | ** | 133 |
| Cleftweave | Stob Coire nam Beith | 450 | II/III | - | Ice | Snow-ice | * | 134 |
| The Pyramid | Stob Coire nam Beith | 90 | III | - | Mixed | General | * | 134 |
| Summit Gully | Stob Coire nam Beith | 500 | II | - | Snow | - | ** | 134 |
| The Chasm of An t-Sròn | Stob Coire nam Beith | 360 | IV | 4 | Ice | Cascade | * | 134 |
| **Glen Coe – outlying areas** | | | | | | | | 135 |
| Quartzvein Scoop | Beinn Udlaidh | 90 | IV | 4 | Ice | Cascade | *** | 137 |
| Captain Hook | Beinn Udlaidh | 75 | VI | 6 | Ice | Cascade | *** | 137 |
| Cut-Throat | Beinn Udlaidh | 75 | VI | 6 | Ice | Cascade | *** | 137 |
| Peter Pan Direct | Beinn Udlaidh | 85 | V | 5 | Ice | Cascade | *** | 139 |
| South Gully of Black Wall | Beinn Udlaidh | 120 | IV | 4 | Ice | Cascade | *** | 139 |
| Ramshead Gully | Beinn Udlaidh | 120 | III | - | Ice | Cascade | * | 139 |

## Winter Climbs: Glen Coe

| Route name | Area | Route length (metres) | Overall grade | Technical grade | Main style | Sub-style(s) | Rating | Page |
|---|---|---|---|---|---|---|---|---|
| Sunshine Gully | Beinn Udlaidh | 90 | III | 3 | Ice | Cascade | *** | 139 |
| Central Gully | Beinn Udlaidh | 180 | II | - | Ice | Cascade |  | 139 |
| Doctor's Dilemma | Beinn Udlaidh | 180 | IV | 4 | Ice | Cascade | ** | 139 |
| Junior's Jangle | Beinn Udlaidh | 90 | IV | 4 | Ice | Cascade | * | 139 |
| West Gully | Beinn Udlaidh | 180 | III | - | Ice | Cascade | ** | 139 |
| Organ Pipe Wall | Beinn Udlaidh | 75 | V | 5 | Ice | Cascade | ** | 142 |
| The Smirk | Beinn Udlaidh | 90 | V | 5 | Ice | Cascade | *** | 142 |
| Red Gully | Sgùrr na h-Ulaidh | 200 | III | - | Ice | Snow-ice | ** | 142 |
| The School House Ridge | Beinn a' Bheithir | 580 | I | - | Mixed | Turf | * | 142 |
| The Dragon's Tooth | Beinn a' Bheithir | 700 | II | - | Mixed | Turf | ** | 142 |
| Rapunzel | Beinn Fhionnlaidh | 350 | IV | - | Ice | Cascade | ** | 144 |
| The Great Ridge | Garbh Bheinn | 300 | IV | 4 | Mixed | Rock, turf | ** | 146 |
| The Great Gully | Garbh Bheinn | 300 | VI | 6 | Ice, mixed | Cascade | ** | 146 |
| Inglis Clark Ridge | Stob a' Ghlais Choire | 140 | III | - | Mixed | General | * | 147 |

# APPENDIX C
## Route summary table by style

| Route name | Area | Route length (metres) | Overall grade | Technical grade | Main style | Sub-style(s) | Rating | Page |
|---|---|---|---|---|---|---|---|---|
| Crowberry Gully | Stob Dearg | 300 | IV | 4 | Ice | Snow-ice | *** | 65 |
| North East Zig-Zag | Stob Dearg | 100 | III | - | Ice | Snow-ice | * | 66 |
| Ephemeron Gully | Stob Dearg | 340 | IV | 4 | Ice | Snow-ice | * | 68 |
| Central Couloir | Stob Coire Altruim | 100 | III | - | Ice | Snow-ice | | 70 |
| Langsam | Stob Coire nan Lochan | 200 | II/III | - | Ice | Snow-ice | *** | 97 |
| Twisting Gully | Stob Coire nan Lochan | 150 | III | 4 | Ice | Snow-ice | ** | 98 |
| SC Gully | Stob Coire nan Lochan | 150 | III | 3 | Ice | Snow-ice | *** | 101 |
| Number Three Gully | West face of Aonach Dubh | 300 | III | - | Ice | Snow-ice | *** | 119 |
| C-D Scoop | West face of Aonach Dubh | 150 | II | - | Ice | Snow-ice | ** | 119 |
| Number Six Gully | West face of Aonach Dubh | 240 | IV | 4 | Ice | Snow-ice | *** | 121 |
| North-West Gully | Stob Coire nam Beith | 500 | III | - | Ice | Snow-ice | ** | 133 |
| Cleftweave | Stob Coire nam Beith | 450 | II/III | - | Ice | Snow-ice | * | 134 |

## WINTER CLIMBS: GLEN COE

| Route name | Area | Route length (metres) | Overall grade | Technical grade | Main style | Sub-style(s) | Rating | Page |
|---|---|---|---|---|---|---|---|---|
| Red Gully | Sgùrr na h-Ulaidh | 200 | III | - | Ice | Snow-ice | ** | 142 |
| Blue Riband | Aonach Eagach | 600 | V | 5 | Ice | Cascade | *** | 54 |
| Chancellor Gully | Aonach Eagach | 500 | III/IV | - | Ice | Cascade | ** | 55 |
| The Chasm | Stob Dearg | 450 | V | 6 | Ice | Cascade | *** | 58 |
| Lady's Gully | Stob Dearg | 240 | IV | 4 | Ice | Cascade | ** | 60 |
| Great Gully | Stob Dearg | 360 | II/III | - | Ice | Cascade | | 68 |
| Eilde Canyon | Sròn na Lairig and Eilde Canyon | 30–40 | IV/V | - | Ice | Cascade | | 73 |
| The Bubble | Sròn na Lairig and Eilde Canyon | 60 | III/IV | 4 | Ice | Cascade | *** | 73 |
| Avalanche Gully | North-west face of Gearr Aonach | 300 | IV | 4 | Ice | Cascade | * | 89 |
| Findlay's Rise | North face of Aonach Dubh | 240 | IV | 5 | Ice | Cascade | * | 111 |
| Elliot's Downfall | West face of Aonach Dubh | 115 | V | 6 | Ice | Cascade | *** | 121 |
| The Corridors | Stob Coire nam Beith | 160 | III/IV | 4 | Ice | Cascade | * | 131 |
| Central Gully | Stob Coire nam Beith | 450 | IV | 4 | Ice | Cascade | ** | 133 |

## Appendix C – Route summary table by style

| Route name | Area | Route length (metres) | Overall grade | Technical grade | Main style | Sub-style(s) | Rating | Page |
|---|---|---|---|---|---|---|---|---|
| The Chasm of An t-Sròn | Stob Coire nam Beith | 360 | IV | 4 | Ice | Cascade | * | 134 |
| Quartzvein Scoop | Beinn Udlaidh | 90 | IV | 4 | Ice | Cascade | *** | 137 |
| Captain Hook | Beinn Udlaidh | 75 | VI | 6 | Ice | Cascade | *** | 137 |
| Cut-Throat | Beinn Udlaidh | 75 | VI | 6 | Ice | Cascade | *** | 137 |
| Peter Pan Direct | Beinn Udlaidh | 85 | V | 5 | Ice | Cascade | *** | 139 |
| South Gully of Black Wall | Beinn Udlaidh | 120 | IV | 4 | Ice | Cascade | *** | 139 |
| Ramshead Gully | Beinn Udlaidh | 120 | III | - | Ice | Cascade | * | 139 |
| Sunshine Gully | Beinn Udlaidh | 90 | III | 3 | Ice | Cascade | *** | 139 |
| Central Gully | Beinn Udlaidh | 180 | II | - | Ice | Cascade | | 139 |
| Doctor's Dilemma | Beinn Udlaidh | 180 | IV | 4 | Ice | Cascade | ** | 139 |
| Junior's Jangle | Beinn Udlaidh | 90 | IV | 4 | Ice | Cascade | * | 139 |
| West Gully | Beinn Udlaidh | 180 | III | - | Ice | Cascade | | 139 |
| Organ Pipe Wall | Beinn Udlaidh | 75 | V | 5 | Ice | Cascade | ** | 142 |
| The Smirk | Beinn Udlaidh | 90 | V | 5 | Ice | Cascade | *** | 142 |
| Rapunzel | Beinn Fhionnlaidh | 350 | IV | - | Ice | Cascade | ** | 144 |
| The Wabe | East face of Gearr Aonach | 135 | V | 5 | Ice | Snow patch cascade | *** | 85 |
| Excellerator | Far Eastern Buttress | 25 | V | 5 | Ice | Snow patch cascade | * | 108 |
| Jane's Weep | Far Eastern Buttress | 25 | VIII | 8 | Ice | Snow patch cascade | * | 108 |

## Winter Climbs: Glen Coe

| Route name | Area | Route length (metres) | Overall grade | Technical grade | Main style | Sub-style(s) | Rating | Page |
|---|---|---|---|---|---|---|---|---|
| The Screen | West face of Aonach Dubh | 75 | IV | 5 | Ice | Snow patch cascade | * | 119 |
| The Great Gully | Garbh Bheinn | 300 | VI | 6 | Ice, mixed | Cascade | ** | 146 |
| Direct Route | Stob Dearg | 95 | IV | - | Mixed | General | * | 60 |
| Kinloss Corner | Stob Dearg | 120 | V | 6 | Mixed | General | ** | 61 |
| Shelf Route | Stob Dearg | 200 | IV | 6 | Mixed | General | ** | 65 |
| Raven's Gully | Stob Dearg | 135 | V | 6 | Mixed | General | *** | 66 |
| Raven's Edge | Stob Dearg | 170 | VII | 7 | Mixed | General | *** | 67 |
| Cuneiform Buttress, Ordinary Route | Stob Dearg | 135 | IV | 5 | Mixed | General | | 67 |
| The Long Chimney | Stob Dearg | 135 | IV | - | Mixed | General | ** | 68 |
| Lagangarbh Chimney | Stob Dearg | 60 | III | 4 | Mixed | General | ** | 68 |
| Chimney Route | Lost Valley Buttresses | 75 | III/IV | 4 | Mixed | General | * | 78 |
| Minor Adjustment | Lost Valley Buttresses | 115 | IV | 5 | Mixed | General | * | 78 |
| Sabre Tooth | Lost Valley Buttresses | 135 | IV | 5 | Mixed | General | * | 78 |
| Directosaur | Lost Valley Buttresses | 160 | VI | 7 | Mixed | General | * | 80 |
| Neanderthal | Lost Valley Buttresses | 125 | VII | 7 | Mixed | General | *** | 81 |

## Appendix C – Route summary table by style

| Route name | Area | Route length (metres) | Overall grade | Technical grade | Main style | Sub-style(s) | Rating | Page |
|---|---|---|---|---|---|---|---|---|
| Barracuda | Lost Valley Buttresses | 80 | V | 7 | Mixed | General | ** | 81 |
| Ingrid's Folly and Peregrine Gully | East face of Gearr Aonach | 300 | III | - | Mixed | General | * | 86 |
| East Face Route | Stob Coire nan Lochan | 130 | VI | 7 | Mixed | General | ** | 101 |
| Fingal's Chimney | North face of Aonach Dubh | 190 | VI | 7 | Mixed | General | *** | 113 |
| Fall-Out | North face of Aonach Dubh | 125 | VII | 7 | Mixed | General | *** | 113 |
| The Crook | Bidean nam Bian | 50 | VI | 7 | Mixed | General |  | 128 |
| Return of the Nedi | Bidean nam Bian | 90 | IV | 5 | Mixed | General | ** | 129 |
| The Gash | Bidean nam Bian | 120 | IV | 4 | Mixed | General | ** | 129 |
| Zero Buttress | Stob Coire nam Beith | 115 | IV | 4 | Mixed | General | * | 131 |
| The Sphinx | Stob Coire nam Beith | 135 | IV | 5 | Mixed | General | ** | 133 |
| The Pyramid | Stob Coire nam Beith | 90 | III | - | Mixed | General | * | 134 |
| Inglis Clark Ridge | Stob a' Ghlais Choire | 140 | III | - | Mixed | General | * | 147 |

## Winter Climbs: Glen Coe

| Route name | Area | Route length (metres) | Overall grade | Technical grade | Main style | Sub-style(s) | Rating | Page |
|---|---|---|---|---|---|---|---|---|
| Right Edge | Lost Valley Buttresses | 120 | IV | 4 | Mixed | Ice | ** | 78 |
| Gully B | East face of Gearr Aonach | 230 | II | - | Mixed | Ice | | 83 |
| Gully A | East face of Gearr Aonach | 235 | IV | 4 | Mixed | Ice | * | 83 |
| Lost Leeper Gully | East face of Gearr Aonach | 300 | III | 4 | Mixed | Ice | ** | 85 |
| Rev Ted's Gully | East face of Gearr Aonach | 300 | III | - | Mixed | Ice | * | 86 |
| Rescue Team Gully | North-west face of Gearr Aonach | 85 | II/III | - | Mixed | Ice | * | 91 |
| Pinnacle Buttress Groove | Stob Coire nan Lochan | 60 | III | - | Mixed | Ice | * | 105 |
| Darwin's Dihedral | North face of Aonach Dubh | 240 | VI | 6 | Mixed | Ice | ** | 111 |
| Venom | North face of Aonach Dubh | 240 | IV/V | 5 | Mixed | Ice | * | 111 |
| White Snake | North face of Aonach Dubh | 240 | IV | 4 | Mixed | Ice | ** | 111 |
| Ossian's Close | North face of Aonach Dubh | 240 | III | - | Mixed | Ice | * | 111 |

## APPENDIX C – ROUTE SUMMARY TABLE BY STYLE

| Route name | Area | Route length (metres) | Overall grade | Technical grade | Main style | Sub-style(s) | Rating | Page |
|---|---|---|---|---|---|---|---|---|
| Midnight Special | North face of Aonach Dubh | 300 | V | 5 | Mixed | Ice | * | 111 |
| Midnight Cowboy | North face of Aonach Dubh | 370 | V | 6 | Mixed | Ice | ** | 112 |
| Amphitheatre Scoop Direct | West face of Aonach Dubh | 240 | V | 5 | Mixed | Ice | *** | 121 |
| Number Four Gully | West face of Aonach Dubh | 300 | IV | 4 | Mixed | Ice | * | 121 |
| North Route | Bidean nam Bian | 210 | III | - | Mixed | Ice | * | 124 |
| Diamond Route | Bidean nam Bian | 255 | V | 6 | Mixed | Ice | * | 124 |
| Direct Route | Bidean nam Bian | 150 | V | 6 | Mixed | Ice | ** | 124 |
| Closer | Bidean nam Bian | 75 | IV | 5 | Mixed | Ice | ** | 129 |
| St Peter's Well | Bidean nam Bian | 50 | VI | 7 | Mixed | Ice | ** | 129 |
| Number One Buttress | Stob Coire nam Beith | 270 | II/III | - | Mixed | Ice | * | 131 |
| Arch Gully | Stob Coire nam Beith | 270 | III | - | Mixed | Ice | * | 131 |
| Deep-Cut Chimney | Stob Coire nam Beith | 450 | IV | 4 | Mixed | Ice | *** | 133 |

## WINTER CLIMBS: GLEN COE

| Route name | Area | Route length (metres) | Overall grade | Technical grade | Main style | Sub-style(s) | Rating | Page |
|---|---|---|---|---|---|---|---|---|
| Rainmaker | East face of Gearr Aonach | 100 | VI | 5 | Mixed | Ice, rock | ** | 85 |
| Mome Rath Face Route | East face of Gearr Aonach | 135 | V | 5 | Mixed | Ice, rock | *** | 85 |
| Scabbard Chimney | Stob Coire nan Lochan | 120 | V | 6 | Mixed | Ice or rock | *** | 96 |
| Spectre | Stob Coire nan Lochan | 120 | V | 6 | Mixed | Ice or rock | ** | 97 |
| Innuendo | Stob Coire nan Lochan | 150 | V | 6 | Mixed | Ice, rock | ** | 97 |
| Against All Odds | North face of Aonach Dubh | 150 | VI/VII | 7 | Mixed | Ice, turf | ** | 113 |
| Middle Ledge | West face of Aonach Dubh | 600 | II | - | Mixed | Ice, turf | | 117 |
| Chimney Route | Stob Coire nan Lochan | 125 | VI | 6 | Mixed | Ice, turf, rock | *** | 100 |
| Aonach Eagach Traverse | Aonach Eagach | 3000 | III | - | Mixed | Rock | *** | 53 |
| North Face Route | Stob Dearg | 220 | V | 6 | Mixed | Rock | ** | 61 |
| D Gully Buttress | Stob Dearg | 150 | IV | 4 | Mixed | Rock | ** | 62 |
| Curved Ridge | Stob Dearg | 300 | III | 3 | Mixed | Rock | *** | 63 |
| Agag's Groove | Stob Dearg | 105 | VII | 7 | Mixed | Rock | *** | 65 |
| Naismith's Route | Stob Dearg | 200 | IV | 5 | Mixed | Rock | * | 65 |
| The Zig-Zags | East face of Gearr Aonach | 200 | II | - | Mixed | Rock | ** | 88 |

## APPENDIX C – ROUTE SUMMARY TABLE BY STYLE

| Route name | Area | Route length (metres) | Overall grade | Technical grade | Main style | Sub-style(s) | Rating | Page |
|---|---|---|---|---|---|---|---|---|
| The Dual | Stob Coire nan Lochan | 133 | IX | 9 | Mixed | Rock | *** | 96 |
| Dorsal Arête | Stob Coire nan Lochan | 120 | II | 3 | Mixed | Rock | *** | 97 |
| Unicorn | Stob Coire nan Lochan | 125 | VIII | 8 | Mixed | Rock | *** | 100 |
| Central Grooves | Stob Coire nan Lochan | 120 | VII | 7 | Mixed | Rock | *** | 101 |
| Central Buttress | Stob Coire nan Lochan | 135 | VII | 7 | Mixed | Rock | *** | 101 |
| Evening Citizen | Stob Coire nan Lochan | 95 | V | 7 | Mixed | Rock | ** | 103 |
| Para Andy | Stob Coire nan Lochan | 90 | VI | 7 | Mixed | Rock | ** | 103 |
| Intruder | Stob Coire nan Lochan | 100 | V | 7 | Mixed | Rock | ** | 104 |
| Crest Route | Stob Coire nan Lochan | 115 | V | 6 | Mixed | Rock | *** | 104 |
| Nirvana Wall | Far Eastern Buttress | 75 | VI | 8 | Mixed | Rock | ** | 108 |
| Yen | Far Eastern Buttress | 100 | VI | 7 | Mixed | Rock | | 108 |
| Dinner-Time Buttress | West face of Aonach Dubh | 335 | II | - | Mixed | Rock | ** | 116 |

## Winter Climbs: Glen Coe

| Route name | Area | Route length (metres) | Overall grade | Technical grade | Main style | Sub-style(s) | Rating | Page |
|---|---|---|---|---|---|---|---|---|
| The Pinnacle Face | West face of Aonach Dubh | 110 | IV | 5 | Mixed | Rock | * | 119 |
| Amphitheatre North Ridge | West face of Aonach Dubh | 100 | II | 3 | Mixed | Rock | ** | 121 |
| Un Poco Loco Direct Direct | Bidean nam Bian | 120 | VII | 7 | Mixed | Rock | ** | 125 |
| Crypt Route | Bidean nam Bian | 60 | IV | 6 | Mixed | Rock | *** | 125 |
| Flake Route, Right Hand | Bidean nam Bian | 190 | V | 7 | Mixed | Rock | ** | 125 |
| Knights Templar | Bidean nam Bian | 150 | VII | 8 | Mixed | Rock | ** | 127 |
| North Buttress | Stob Dearg | 300 | IV | 4 | Mixed | Rock or ice | *** | 66 |
| Pterodactyl (Moonlight Gully) | Lost Valley Buttresses | 110 | V | 6/7 | Mixed | Rock, ice | * | 80 |
| Moonlighting | Lost Valley Buttresses | 120 | V | 6 | Mixed | Rock, turf | * | 81 |
| The Great Ridge | Garbh Bheinn | 300 | IV | 4 | Mixed | Rock, turf | ** | 146 |
| Vice Chancellor Ridge | Aonach Eagach | 210 | III | - | Mixed | Turf | ** | 54 |
| The Chancellor | Aonach Eagach | 400 | IV | - | Mixed | Turf | ** | 54 |
| Bodach Buttress | Aonach Eagach | 120 | III | 4 | Mixed | Turf | * | 55 |
| Alpen | Stob Dearg | 245 | V | 5 | Mixed | Turf | * | 61 |
| Route I | Stob Dearg | 70 | V | 6 | Mixed | Turf | * | 63 |
| Dalmation Couloir | Stob Coire Altruim | 100 | IV | - | Mixed | Turf | *** | 70 |

## Appendix C – Route summary table by style

| Route name | Area | Route length (metres) | Overall grade | Technical grade | Main style | Sub-style(s) | Rating | Page |
|---|---|---|---|---|---|---|---|---|
| Sròn na Lairig | Sròn na Lairig and Eilde Canyon | 300 | II | - | Mixed | Turf | ** | 71 |
| 999 | North-west face of Gearr Aonach | 135 | IV | 5 | Mixed | Turf | ** | 91 |
| Ordinary Route | Stob Coire nan Lochan | 130 | IV | 5 | Mixed | Turf | ** | 95 |
| Twisting Grooves | Stob Coire nan Lochan | 130 | IV | 5 | Mixed | Turf | ** | 98 |
| Moonshadow | Stob Coire nan Lochan | 150 | IV | 5 | Mixed | Turf | ** | 100 |
| Tilt | Stob Coire nan Lochan | 140 | VI | 7 | Mixed | Turf | *** | 100 |
| Orient Express | Far Eastern Buttress | 85 | IV | 5 | Mixed | Turf | * | 106 |
| Eastern Slant | Far Eastern Buttress | 120 | III | 4 | Mixed | Turf | * | 106 |
| Cyclops | West face of Aonach Dubh | 105 | IV | 5 | Mixed | Turf | * | 117 |
| The School House Ridge | Beinn a' Bheithir | 580 | I | - | Mixed | Turf | * | 142 |
| The Dragon's Tooth | Beinn a' Bheithir | 700 | II | - | Mixed | Turf | ** | 142 |

## WINTER CLIMBS: GLEN COE

| Route name | Area | Route length (metres) | Overall grade | Technical grade | Main style | Sub-style(s) | Rating | Page |
|---|---|---|---|---|---|---|---|---|
| Outgrabe Route | East face of Gearr Aonach | 115 | V | 5 | Mixed | Turf, ice | ** | 85 |
| Raeburn's Route | Stob Coire nan Lochan | 150 | IV | 4 | Mixed | Turf, ice | *** | 103 |
| West Chimney Route | Bidean nam Bian | 180 | V | 6 | Mixed | Turf, ice | *** | 127 |
| Gully C | East face of Gearr Aonach | 230 | I | - | Snow | - |  | 83 |
| Boomerang Gully | Stob Coire nan Lochan | 210 | II | - | Snow | - | * | 95 |
| Broad Gully | Stob Coire nan Lochan | 150 | I | - | Snow | - | * | 97 |
| Forked Gully | Stob Coire nan Lochan | 135 | I/II | - | Snow | - | * | 98 |
| NC Gully | Stob Coire nan Lochan | 155 | II | - | Snow | - | ** | 103 |
| North Gully | Stob Coire nan Lochan | 75 | I/II | - | Snow | - |  | 105 |
| Central Gully | Bidean nam Bian | 180 | I or II | - | Snow | - | ** | 125 |
| Hourglass Gully | Bidean nam Bian | 120 | I | - | Snow | - |  | 129 |
| Summit Gully | Stob Coire nam Beith | 500 | II | - | Snow | - | ** | 134 |
| The Chasm to Crowberry Traverse | Stob Dearg | 1000 | II | - | Snow, mixed | - | * | 60 |

# NOTES

# CICERONE

Trust Cicerone to guide your next adventure, wherever it may be around the world...

Discover guides for hiking, mountain walking, backpacking, trekking, trail running, cycling and mountain biking, ski touring, climbing and scrambling in Britain, Europe and worldwide.

**Connect with Cicerone online and find inspiration.**

- buy books and ebooks
- articles, advice and trip reports
- podcasts and live events
- GPX files and updates
- regular newsletter

**cicerone.co.uk**

# NOTES

# CICERONE

Trust Cicerone to guide your next adventure, wherever it may be around the world...

Discover guides for hiking, mountain walking, backpacking, trekking, trail running, cycling and mountain biking, ski touring, climbing and scrambling in Britain, Europe and worldwide.

### Connect with Cicerone online and find inspiration.

- buy books and ebooks
- articles, advice and trip reports
- podcasts and live events
- GPX files and updates
- regular newsletter

### cicerone.co.uk

# NOTES

# CICERONE

Trust Cicerone to guide your next adventure, wherever it may be around the world...

Discover guides for hiking, mountain walking, backpacking, trekking, trail running, cycling and mountain biking, ski touring, climbing and scrambling in Britain, Europe and worldwide.

**Connect with Cicerone online and find inspiration.**

- buy books and ebooks
- articles, advice and trip reports
- podcasts and live events
- GPX files and updates
- regular newsletter

**cicerone.co.uk**